"Megha is a master at evoking the elixir of life. In this book, *Expanding Joy*, she lovingly introduces you to the embodied joy that is Let Your Yoga Dance."

—Don Stapleton, PhD, Cofounder, Nosara Yoga Institute, author of *Self-Awakening Yoga: The Expansion of Consciousness through the Body's Own Wisdom.*

"*Expanding Joy* is personal, intellectual, authoritative, and fun. I love the way Megha shines through the words. It was a privilege reading this!"

—Fiona Trembath, writer, Positive Psychologist Melbourne, Australia

"What a wonderful offering! Megha Nancy Buttenheim combines yoga, dance, spirituality, psychology, and healthy movement breaks to show us how to embody joy, open the heart, and deepen our connection to life. *Expanding Joy: Let Your Yoga Dance* is both exhilarating and profound."

—James Baraz, co-founding teacher of Spirit Rock Meditation Center, author of *Awakening Joy.*

"Megha holds a clear view and a transparent excitement for her work that is deftly transferred to her students. She brings to these pages sentiments that will enthrall, entertain, and enlighten the reader on what it means to dance your yoga."

—Vinn Arjuna Martí, founder of Soul Motion

Expanding Joy

Let Your Yoga Dance

EMBODYING POSITIVE PSYCHOLOGY

by Megha Nancy Buttenheim, MA, E-RYT 1000
Founding Director, *Let Your Yoga Dance*®

Foreword by Dr. Tal Ben-Shahar
Preface by Megan McDonough

Dedication:

To Susan Robertson, my oldest, dearest friend. You left us too soon, my beloved twin. Eternal love to you.

and to

Patricia Peterson, my modern dance teacher from high school who taught me everything I needed to learn about being a professional—in performance, in teaching, in living.

Grace in Motion Books
4205 Castle Bridge Lane, Suite # 1112
Sarasota, Fl 34238 USA

Videographer for Let's Move Takeaways: Rick Sands
Front and Back Cover Photography: Pan Trinity Das
Web Mastermind for Takeaways and Links: George Cieszka
Author Photography: Robert Longley
Book Design: Nathan Lawton

Expanding Joy
Let Your Yoga Dance
Embodying Positive Psychology

ISBN-13: 978-0692622292 (Custom Universal)
ISBN-10: 0692622292
BISAC: Body, Mind & Spirit / General

Content

Foreword

by Dr. Tal Ben-Shahar

author of *Happier* and *Choose the Life You Want*

The eminent psychologist Carl Rogers wrote, "What is most personal is most general." Following his wise words, I would like to share what has been, and still is, most personal for me in my encounter with Let Your Yoga Dance.

Throughout my first Let Your Yoga Dance class, my head was spinning—not because of any fancy dance moves, but because I recognized the potential in what Megha was doing for my own and others' happiness. Dance and music, in and of themselves, contribute to joy. When these are combined with a deep grounding in Eastern philosophy and psychology, as well as Western scientific work, then the outcome is a radical expansion of joy. It is this radical expansion of joy that Megha inspires in me and in thousands of others who have had the privilege of learning from her or from her students.

This book can and ought to revolutionize the way we think and practice psychology, in that it brings a missing component to the field. Until recently, psychology has focused primarily on the mind, on the cognitive, and has largely neglected the body, the physical. In this book, Megha seamlessly merges mind and body, the cognitive and the physical, thus becoming a pioneer in the emerging field of embodied psychology.

In a most wonderful way, a Let Your Yoga Dance class is both attentive and indifferent to how I feel. Attentive, in that the class meets me however I am feeling, and immediately embraces my emotional state. Indifferent, in that regardless of whatever feelings I might have, I am led to a place of joy. The joy either augments what I was already feeling, or it functions as a healing force for any emotional pain I might have been experiencing.

Let Your Yoga Dance changed—and continues to change—my life for the better, to the point where I cannot see my life without it. And now, it thrills me to no end that, through this book, more people will be exposed to Megha's teachings.

Best wishes,

Tal Ben-Shahar

Preface

by Megan McDonough
author of *Radically Receptive Meditation*

In this book, Megha Nancy Buttenheim invites you to use your body to understand happiness, gratitude, grace, and love not just as intellectual concepts, but in a much deeper way. Comparing ancient yoga traditions to modern psychological science, Megha merges Eastern and Western perspectives to propose a whole-body approach to thriving.

Through a blend of personal stories, the science of positive psychology, the wisdom of yoga, and short try-it-for-yourself movements and breathing exercises, readers experience and explore how happiness grows in an embodied way.

I began working with Megha when she joined the faculty for the inaugural Certificate in Positive Psychology course. Her role was, and still is, to take key learning concepts and help students live them from the inside out—to dance the lessons, if you will. After 30 years of teaching, Megha knew this body-centered approach would work to enliven the learning. The rest of us—faculty and students alike—were a bit more tentative. Those of us who had experienced Megha's work in the past, including Tal and me, knew that it had the power to transform your state of mind. But, we wondered, would 180 students, who had signed up to learn positive psychology, "get it"?

Turns out, the answer was—and is—a resounding yes. This innocent and lively play-in and workout is more than a fun activity, though it certainly is fun. The movement deeply changes people's relationship to the material, and more importantly, to themselves. Let Your Yoga Dance for Embodied Positive Psychology is now a cornerstone of the program, bringing alive a felt sense of human flourishing.

Our students in the yearlong CiPP course have Megha right there in person teaching Let Your Yoga Dance techniques to support them in connecting with others, growing in joy, and experiencing a lighthearted playfulness. Now you, too, dear reader, can reap the benefits of this beautiful approach.

Wishing you all the best, always,

Megan McDonough
CEO, Wholebeing Institute

"Re-examine all you have been told in school or church or in any book, and dismiss whatever insults your own soul; and your very flesh shall be a great poem, and have the richest fluency, not only in words, but in the silent lines of its lips and face and between the lashes of your eyes, and in every motion and joint of your body."

—Walt Whitman, *Leaves of Grass*, preface, xxvii

Important: Please Read

Weaving throughout this book are fourteen movement breaks. Each one explores either breathing techniques, yoga movements, chakra dancing, guided visualization, or meditation, all under the heading: **LET'S MOVE Takeaways**

Step 1) To Download:

As a reader of this book, you have been given a coupon code to access a free download of all the Takeaway videos. The Takeaways can be found at the store on my Let Your Yoga Dance website: store.letyouryogadance.com. The title of the coupon code is: **FREETAKEAWAY**

Step 2) To Stream videos on-line:

After you have created an account on the Let Your Yoga Dance Store and redeemed the coupon for the Takeaways, you will have access to view the videos on the store website. You can click to view these videos directly at the store. You must complete **Step 1) To Download** to establish restricted access to the video streams.

Disclaimer regarding Takeaways

Understand that when participating in any movement experience, there is the possibility of physical injury. If you engage in the movement Takeaways, you agree that you are voluntarily participating, and are doing so at your own risk. Your body is the boss, not me. Make sure to obey your body; you can always modify my guidance.

Enjoy!

Introduction

I've got some great news:

You are a dancer.

Even if you've been a couch potato, are a computer geek, or have been physically challenged your entire life, you're still a dancer. You might not be a professional dancer, but you're a dancer, nonetheless; it's your birthright.

Your body is more than something to keep your head portable.

Have you noticed that little kids running about are fully embodied, but many grown-ups are talking heads? What about the brilliance of our knees, toes, ankles, elbows...not to mention our fabulous fascia, the connective tissue? The time has come to marvel at our magical, mysterious, magnificent bodies!

Expanding your joy is possible.

It might take some concentrated effort and work on your part, but you can, in fact, expand your joy. We humans have tremendous opportunities to become happier. This book, guided by Let Your Yoga Dance, can show you how!

Welcome to Expanding Joy Let Your Yoga Dance
EMBODYING POSITIVE PSYCHOLOGY

I have written this book to share four things with you:

1. Let Your Yoga Dance and our mission: to spread joy and consciousness throughout the world by transmitting body health, brain health, heart health, and soul health to all populations.

2. Positive Psychology and the merging of this powerful science with Let Your Yoga Dance.

3. The SPIRE model of whole-person well-being.

4. Healthy takeaway tools for you to use and enjoy while reading, or to use anytime.

Definitions

Sometimes you will come across phrases and words from various traditions—including the dance world, the yoga world, the theater world, and Positive Psychology—which might seem foreign to a newcomer. I'll translate these expressions as I go along.

Introduction to LET'S MOVE and the AWARENESS PAUSE

Because this book is a love song to the human body, I have sprinkled Let Your Yoga Dance movements, yoga exercises, and breath techniques throughout so that you can receive an infusion of energy as you read.

Most of them take just two to three minutes to practice. Did you know that every 90 minutes or so, we experience ultradian dips? As Sonja Lyubomirsky mentions in *The Myths of Happiness*, these are times of lethargy, possible negativity, and fatigue that last about twenty minutes. Contained within these pages is a helpful antidote: Fourteen LET'S MOVE Takeaways, your personal ultradian dip blasters!

We have at our fingertips (or I should say, at the tip of our nose) a wonderful gift: our breath. Why not take three deep breaths right now? Many of us have assumed since childhood that learning is about sitting at a desk or in a large hall, listening to a teacher expound, or reading from textbooks for hours. I don't know about you, but in my grammar school, high school, and college, we were never asked to stand up, take a stretch break, and honor the body while learning all that important material. We had sports in the afternoon, but, for the most part, we sat at those desks hour after hour.

In this book, you'll be asked occasionally to push the Pause button on your reading experience. You will be given a little physical task, called either LET'S MOVE or AWARENESS PAUSE. Hopefully, this will result in more energy and focus, and a much happier, alert mind and body. I have named the energy building tasks Energy Boosters. Movements that are calming and sustaining are called Energy Balancers.

Let's begin right now: After reading the directions on the next page, either remain seated or come to standing. Try on this first takeaway:

LET'S MOVE!
Takeaway 1
Energy Balancer

"Ha" Breaths: Coordinating Breath with Movement

One helpful energy balancer is to breathe in through the nose and out through the mouth on an audible sigh—a "ha" sound.

- Take three long breaths in and out. Inhale through the nostrils, and exhale through the mouth with an audible sigh. Each time you exhale on a "ha" sound, you release stale air from the bottom of the lungs, which then opens the lungs to receive fresh oxygen and more energy.

- Now begin to incorporate movement: As you inhale, gently raise your arms out to the side. Halfway up, turn the palms up and move the arms as far overhead as is comfortable for you.

- Turn your palms out, and exhale your arms back down by your side. Repeat four more times. By including the arms in this way, you are coordinating breath with movement.

Now that your body has received a well-deserved awareness and movement moment, notice what's happening. Does your breath feel more expansive? Does your mind feel more alert? Does your body feel more alive?

Research Validates Let Your Yoga Dance!

I am delighted that research studies are emerging that validate everything about the body and dance that I have witnessed throughout my three-plus decades of teaching. Until the twenty-first century, I was relying on fantastic anecdotal evidence. But now there is documented scientific evidence proving what the dancers, yogis, meditators, including His Holiness the Dalai Lama, have known for centuries: the body and the brain are malleable. They continuously learn and grow—if used properly and treated well! Neuroscientists have been studying the beneficial effects of dance on the brain, as well as the body and mind.

Did you know that dancing can make us smarter? A major study by the Albert Einstein College of Medicine in New York City, published in the *New England Journal of Medicine* and funded by the National Institute on Aging, revealed that by stimulating cognitive activity, dancing can help ward off Alzheimer's disease and other forms of dementia.
(Verghese et al.)

Research has also shown that dancing has a powerful impact on boosting happiness, combating stress and depression, and lifting overall mental health. These were the findings of a Swedish study published in the *Archives of Pediatrics & Adolescent Medicine* in which researchers studied 112 teenage girls who were battling issues such anxiety, depression, and stress.
(Duberg et al.)

CHAPTER 1:

What Is
Let Your Yoga Dance?

Let Your Yoga Dance, Defined

Let Your Yoga Dance is a moving celebration of spirit. It's a dance-yoga fusion, using music from all around the world. It's a practice that literally anyone can do, because it's offered in a safe, kind, compassionate environment. Students are invited to move in ways that feel good to them, without pushing too far outside their comfort zone.

Grace and Joy: The Core Values of Let Your Yoga Dance

G - Grounding into Mother Earth, and the earth of your body

R – Releasing into the dance of gentle, kind, moving yoga

A – Aligning into support of self and community

C – Connecting through moving metta, loving-kindness

E – Ecstatic embrace of the dance of body-mind-heart-soul

J – Joy practiced on and off the Let Your Yoga Dance floor

O – Observing with compassion the dancer that you are

Y – Yama and niyama (ethical conduct) practices to support congruent living

How Let Your Yoga Dance Came to Be

Back in the 1980s, when I was an actress and dancer living in Manhattan, I decided to spend the month of August at a holistic health center and yoga ashram, Kripalu Center for Yoga & Health, in the Berkshires of western Massachusetts. I was particularly delighted with three things I discovered at Kripalu: a moving meditative yoga practice; a "spiritual aerobics" class called DansKinetics that welcomed all abilities; and a chance to immerse myself 24/7 in a spiritual lifestyle. That month turned into twelve years. I joined the faculty after my first year, teaching classes and workshops in yoga and dance. I wanted to bring together my three great loves: dance, yoga, and the chakras—the body's energy centers—to create a practice that reminds people at a visceral level, that we are all dancers. For more than a decade, I led retreats and teacher trainings in yoga, holistic health, and my unique form of "dancing yoga."

As a lifelong dancer, I had my own insecurities about whether I was good enough, whether I was thin enough, whether I was talented enough. The dance culture can be demanding, and especially tough for girls and women. Dancing in New York City was challenging and sometimes downright shaming due to the grueling audition processes and expectations regarding physical perfection. The only "great" bodies seemed to be inhabited by taut ballet dancers with their long, lithe limbs elegantly floating up to the sky.

The only Broadway show I ever auditioned for was *A Chorus Line*. I knew I wouldn't get a part because ballet was never my forté. At the audition, held at the beautiful Shubert Theatre, I was instructed to stand on the famous line itself, say my name, and perform one triple pirouette. I could only do a rather sad double. The audition lasted about thirty seconds; I exited stage left with my proverbial tail between my legs. But, hey! There was a silver lining to that cloud of rejection: it was thrilling to just step out on that line, center stage at the Shubert! This was the very place where my theater dreams had begun when, at age seven, I saw my first Broadway musical, *The Flower Drum Song*.

I kept on auditioning, occasionally getting roles in Shakespeare plays and commercials, until I heard an unmistakable siren call wafting from the north, from the Berkshires, that summer long ago.

Then Came Kripalu

Everything changed. Why? Because Kripalu was welcoming. Dancing at Kripalu was fun. No one was turned away from the yoga space or the dance floor, no matter their ability, body type, gender, or age. Living at Kripalu, immersed in karma yoga (selfless service), allowed me to develop and teach that which was true to me. One amazing thing was that I was given free rein to develop my own style. No one was peering over my shoulder. I led thousands of programs over the decades and was never told to lead something else, or do "me" differently. My own style emerged from that original DansKinetics mantle. Living for so many years at the ashram, I wanted my dance to be far more rooted in the depths of yoga. DansKinetics didn't go far enough for me. I kept digging and planting, dancing late at night in one of the many huge program rooms after most ashram residents had gone to bed. Eventually, my unique blend of dancing yoga emerged and blossomed.

The ashram evolved into a nonprofit retreat center in 1995, and my work continued to evolve as well as I followed my calling to create my own school and business. Today, Let Your Yoga Dance is going strong, more confident and more graceful than ever. It has become a worldwide community with hundreds of instructors reaching wider populations. We offer Let Your Yoga Dance trainings, as well as classes for elders, for people with Parkinson's and other chronic conditions, for kids and teens, and for those studying and practicing Positive Psychology. Nowadays, Let Your Yoga Dance is not only my physical and spiritual practice, a community of teachers and practitioners—it is also my dharma, my path.

Reverence for the Body

Sometimes I'm asked, "what's the most important thing you've learned from your three decades of teaching body-based practices?" One of the many things that stand out for me is this: the whole body needs to be respected and revered.

I have discovered that the body is not an afterthought, something to rev up during a dance class or quiet down during a yoga relaxation. The body itself can be the entry point, the alpha and the omega. Therefore, learning beneath a kinesthetic umbrella is a powerful tool that can greatly enhance, land, and launch the teachings of any subject—on health, on Positive Psychology, on life itself!

LET'S MOVE!
Takeaway 2

Breath of Joy
Energy Booster

There are many great tools at your disposal that incorporate breath and movement, which can enliven the spirit and keep the effects of stress and anxiety at bay. Here's one that I especially love:

- Come to a standing position. Inhale through the nose—a quick, sharp sniff—as you bring your arms forward to heart level.

- Now sniff in again, sweeping both arms out to the sides.

- Now sniff a third time, raising your arms overhead.

- As you exhale on a big "ha" sound, bend your knees and drop your arms and torso toward the floor. Go only as far as is comfortable and appropriate for you. If necessary, you can even stay vertical the entire time.

- Come back upright, and repeat the sequence.

- Do this as many time as feels good to you, building up to one minute.

This little moment of deeper breathing accompanied by movement will pull more energy into your body.

Why is it called the Breath of Joy? Notice what happens to your posture when you do these breaths in this way. You are lengthening and lifting through the spine while breathing deeply. Linking these movements and breaths together can result in a joy boost.

Let Your Yoga Dance
Mission and Name

Let's return to the Let Your Yoga Dance mission, which is to spread joy and consciousness throughout the world by transmitting body health, brain health, heart health, and soul health to all populations.

The practice contains four special words. Each one matters; each one is important:

LET   YOUR   YOGA   DANCE

The word **LET** means that you allow the wisdom of your body to flow naturally and easily. Nothing should hurt; there is no need to push or strive.

The word **YOUR** reminds you that this practice is your unique dance of yoga, not mine or anyone else's. You are in charge of your experience. You allow the practice to become a part of you.

This practice is steeped in the time-honored tradition of **YOGA**, particularly the yamas and niyamas—yogic codes of conduct and ethics. Let Your Yoga Dance, born out of yoga, is not only a movement practice, but a spiritual practice as well.

The word **DANCE** describes that which happens when we allow ourselves to be literally moved—physically, heartfully, soulfully—beyond our ingrained habits and self-limiting beliefs. We shed unwanted layers by dancing into our truest selves.

In Let Your Yoga Dance, you come home to the self and return to the soul; you fall in love with your body and experience community in a safe and sacred setting. You use the experience of joy in movement to tone muscles, build flexibility, gain endurance, and increase fitness. This is a healing practice that anyone can do, even someone in a wheelchair or a hospital bed.

Let Your Yoga Dance is sometimes wild and filled with abandon, sometimes a quiet meditation in motion, sometimes completely still. It allows you to reach for the deeper source of energy within. This practice is a beautiful journey that takes you beyond your limitations into contact with grace and your vast spirit.

What Actually Happens When You Let Your Yoga Dance?

A Let Your Yoga Dance experience is like the arc of a rainbow. Seven energy centers provide the basis for this dance of yoga. First, you feel the grounding force of the earth in your feet, legs, and tailbone. Spiraling upward through the element of water, you dance into the sacrum and pelvis, acknowledging the sexy, the sensual, the pleasurable. Traveling still further upward to the ribs and solar plexus, you experience the element of fire: power, strength, and energy. Further upward, in the center of the heart, you dance the element of air: compassion, healing, and loving-kindness. Next, you blast into sweaty intensity with unbridled bliss, finding new levels of self-expression in the throat center. At this point, as the energy moves up to the third eye, the place of witness, the chakra arc of the rainbow starts to descend. You quiet down into a Dance Prayer of moving yoga, gently inviting your wild, extroverted expression back home to your introspective core. Lastly, in the seventh center of energy at the crown of your head, you discover meditation in motion, followed by relaxation. You feel the pulse of your heart, the vast silence of the mind, at one with your multidimensional Self. You lie down and rest, feeling the grounding support of Mother Earth beneath you. After relaxation, you return to seated meditation, ending in stillness, as you began.

A core experience in Let Your Yoga Dance is the ancient practice of metta, or loving-kindness. At certain points in the class, students are invited to send Moving Metta around the room, offering blessings and compassion to fellow group members, and then to their loved ones. Body-based awareness and conscious breathing bring yoga and Let Your Yoga Dance together, making this experience a meditation in motion.

What are the differences between Let Your Yoga Dance and a regular yoga class? A Let Your Yoga Dance class builds intentional community due to the moving connection between dancers. Sometimes group members are divided into partners, trios, and quartets; sometimes everyone faces into the center so that all group members can see each other and be seen. In most yoga classes, students look at a fellow student's back. In a typical Let Your Yoga Dance session, we look into one another's eyes; we look into one another's hearts; we look into one another's souls. A Let Your Yoga Dance class will send people flying about the room with wild, spontaneous creativity. Yoga can cultivate quiet joy, whereas Let Your Yoga Dance also offers outward exuberance!

The Three Health-Promoting Elements of Dance

Peter Lovatt is a principle lecturer at the University of Hertfordshire in England whose interest is in dance and Parkinson's disease. He asks, "Why dance? How can dance help us?" Studies at his university revealed that there are three elements of dancing that improve health:

1. Social (being with others)
2. Physical (heart rate)
3. Cognitive (problem solving)

When you engage these three areas, your body health, brain health, and heart health will improve. Studies have shown that the hippocampus (the part of the brain primarily associated with memory and spatial navigation) actually grows with physical exercise. Let Your Yoga Dance consistently works with cognition, heart rate, and the dance of community.
(See Peter Lovatt's TED Talk on dance and the mind.)

Let's take a few moments to pause, breathe, and quiet the mind.

When we slow down the breath by breathing through the nose, we gradually activate the parasympathetic nervous system, the relaxation response in the body. Soon, the anxious mind will start to calm down. Over the decades in my practice with conscious breathing, I have discovered that **fear and breath cannot live in the same place**.

Let's try it now.

AWARENESS PAUSE
Takeaway 3

Slow, Conscious Nostril Breathing
Energy Balancer

- Slowing the breath down, begin to breathe completely through the nostrils.

- Close your eyes. Sitting tall yet relaxed, invite your mind to follow the rise and fall of your breath.

- How slowly can you breathe? Notice the gap between the exhalation and the next inhalation.

- Can you expand that gap a little bit?

- Invite the mind to befriend the breath, noticing nuance. Let the mind become fascinated with the subtle act of breathing in and out. Even two or three minutes will make a difference.

- Explore this moment of slowing down, breathing quietly and consciously through the nostrils.

The Four Key Elements of Let Your Yoga Dance

Body Health

Let Your Yoga Dance is a terrific workout and play-in. With user-friendly movement, you dance your yoga and you sweat like crazy, keeping your body active, healthy, and alive. When we play in and exercise the body, joy is often an added benefit. Research nowadays warns us that being a couch potato is as dangerous as smoking. The body is our dearest friend. Attention must be paid. It needs to move!

Brain Health

Research shows that the brain can grow throughout a lifetime. Following steps and learning choreography are surefire ways to keep the brain sharp, no matter what the age or ability of the practitioner.

Heart Health

The heart is a muscle, but it is also the seat of love, compassion, and devotion. In Let Your Yoga Dance, not only does the heart get a great aerobic workout, it also opens up emotionally to the self and to others. Let Your Yoga Dance can be helpful for those dealing with depression, because as the heart pulses, it grows, opens, expands. You and your heart dance into community with others and their hearts, and all our hearts begin to pulse as one. Often, for a moment in time, a mini-family is created.

Soul Health

How does Let Your Yoga Dance define soul health? Soul health means being connected to self, to other, to the great mystery of life and beyond. Soul health is the great Dance of Life that goes deeper than the physical body. During class, dancers often become kids again, dancing their yoga in a state of innocence. Soul health is introduced most specifically toward the end of each Let Your Yoga Dance class. As the music becomes quieter and softer, dancers move into meditation in motion, then lie on the ground (or sit in a chair, if needed), taking deep rest in Savasana, the final resting pose. Sometimes folks cry at this point, integrating the benefits of the practice. I think of these tears as the soul singing her song. As the class concludes, everyone quietly sits together in meditation. My intention is that by the time the class is complete, we have brought body, mind, spirit, heart, and soul together in union: yoga.

AWARENESS PAUSE
Takeaway 4

Seated Relaxation: Body Scan
Energy Balancer

- After reading about Savasana, the resting pose, consider putting your book down on your lap and closing your eyes for just two minutes. Sit quietly and notice how you are feeling. Notice the quality of your breath. Is it relaxed or ragged? Simply observe the breath as it flows in and flows out.

- Feel free to experiment with a brief body scan, starting with the feet. Bring your attention all the way down to the feet, noticing how they feel. Send your feet some kind, grateful thoughts. Next, move up to the heels, then the ankles, the lower legs, the knees. Gradually, you will scan your way all the way up to the crown of the head. If you wish to have a longer experience with this awareness pause, scan the front body on the way up to the head, and then scan down the back body, all the way back to the feet.

- As you move through the body with your mind's eye, you might quietly (or inwardly) recite a short affirmation: "My hands are relaxed ... My shoulders are relaxed ... My face is relaxed ... My mind is relaxed ..."

CHAPTER 2:

The Chakras

Life is short. Go dancing, whether it is with flabby arms, or with your muscles, but dance and sing, experience flow!

—Tal Ben-Shahar, Co-founder, Happier TV

Exploring the Chakras

The word *chakra* means "wheel." In the yoga tradition, the chakras represent the seven energy centers of the body, spinning currents that relate to the different elements. Although invisible to the naked eye, the chakras are said to reside within and around the physical body, flowing upward from the base of the spine to the crown of the head.

The chakras provide us with an energy roadmap with which to study ourselves. In their book *The Sevenfold Journey: Reclaiming Mind, Body, and Spirit through the Chakras*, Anodea Judith and Selene Vega compare the chakras to computer memory that stores the basic hardware and functions of our lives. They describe the chakras as "spinning vortices of energy" based around and radiating out from the nerves of the spinal column.

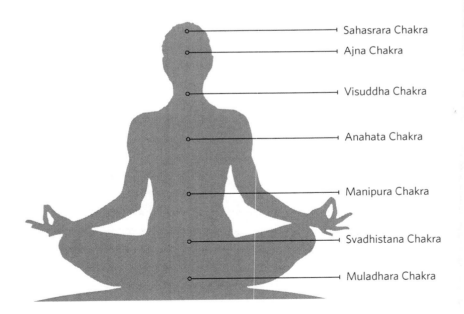

Sahasrara Chakra

Ajna Chakra

Visuddha Chakra

Anahata Chakra

Manipura Chakra

Svadhistana Chakra

Muladhara Chakra

The Seven Chakras

Chakra 1: Muladhara

* Relates to the earth and solid matter; to alignment, safety, security

* Location: Base of the spine, the tailbone. In Let Your Yoga Dance, the feet and legs are included as the root within this chakra.

Dancing with Chakra 1

Planting our feet into Mother Earth is the beginning. Without the grounding force of the muladhara chakra, we cannot live authentically on the earth. Instead, we will reside in the head. Try this: Stand in Mountain pose, with the feet firmly planted beneath you. Raise your arms as far overhead as is comfortable for you. Enjoy the sensation of being rooted in the ground, standing in your authentic self. Notice how you feel.

Chakra 2: Svadhisthana

* Relates to water; birth, sensuality, sexuality, pleasure

* Location: Sacrum, womb, genitals

Dancing with Chakra 2

This chakra reminds us that we are watery, fluid beings. We are eighty percent water: that's a lot! Nowadays, it seems as though people forget that our birthright is a fluid one. The second chakra helps us remember the hips, pelvis, and sacrum. Activities such as hula hooping, belly dancing, and Latin dancing can help us get "down and dirty" in the hips, freeing up long-held physical/emotional tensions. The Let Your Yoga Dance mantra, or repeated phrase, is "I love my belly! I love my butt!" Over the decades, that little phrase has been passed on to children and grandchildren around the world. Hopefully this cultural war against the body will stop. Try it right now:

LET'S MOVE!
Takeaway 5

I Love My Belly, I Love My Butt!
Energy Booster

This takeaway is a core feature of Let Your Yoga Dance when we dance in the second chakra, the watery pelvic, sacral center. "I love my belly, I love my butt" is one of our Let Your Yoga Dance mantras. It works if you work it!

- With loose fists, start gently pounding your pelvis. Pounding the pelvis is actually a martial art technique known as T'an Dien Drumming.

- As you softly pound your pelvis, look down and see if you have said mean things to this part of your anatomy. Your body has received every mental, verbal message you have ever given it. So, if you have been unkind and thoughtless in the past, please say, "I'm sorry," followed by, "I love my belly!" Repeat over and over. If you don't believe the mantra, simply fake it 'til you make it.

- Then start politely pounding your backside and apologize to your butt if you have complained that it doesn't look thin enough, even though you might have given birth to three children.

- After apologizing, start to repeat: "I love my butt."

- After a few repetitions, put it all together. As you pound the pelvis, say, "I love my belly!" As you pound the backside, say, "I love my butt!"

This activity not only stimulates energy, it also gives the body a well-deserved bath of good wishes. And it's funny so you might give yourself a good laugh. We can't get enough humor in this world!

Chakra 3: Manipura

- Relates to fire; strength, power, authority, aggression, resilience
- Location: Solar plexus

Dancing with Chakra 3

This chakra is crucial when we need a boost of power in our lives. Before teaching or before talking with a difficult person, I might move into Warrior pose—bringing one leg forward and bending the knee while keeping the back leg straight. When I sustain this pose for a few breaths, everything starts to change! My body heats up. My breath starts to deepen. The power hormone testosterone increases. I feel stronger and more ready to face my world.

Speaking of power, check out Amy Cuddy's wonderful Ted Talk on Power Poses. She directed research studies proving that testosterone, our power hormone, can rise when we strike a pose as simple as holding the arms overhead for two minutes. At the same time, levels of cortisol (the stress hormone) can decrease!

(www.ted.com/talks/amy_cuddy_your_body_language_shapes_who_you_are)

Let Your Yoga Dance is energy in motion. Dancing our yoga allows us to release old emotions and limiting beliefs. When we dance in our power center, the solar plexus, we discover a new sense of strength and resilience, which in turn facilitates the creation of fresh, empowering emotions. This newfound energy is then free to blast upward from the solar plexus right into the heart, the Anahata Chakra.

Chakra 4: Anahata

- Relates to air; represents the heart of devotion and compassion; the bridge between the first three chakras and the next three chakras.
- Location: Heart

Dancing with Chakra 4

Find a piece of music that resonates with you and dance around the room. A fun Chakra 4 song to use is : "The Sound" by The 1975. Reach your arms out to the side, as if you were embracing the world. Bring the world into your big heart, sending out love and beauty. Start to move quicker, building energy and heat. Get that heart pumping. Who needs some extra compassion today? A war-torn country? Your cousin? The president? Your dog? The five-year-old still living inside you? Refugees yearning to be safe? Dance some love into them all, and smile at them while you dance.

Chakra 5: Visuddha

- Relates to ether and represents sound and truth, self-expression, communication, joy, creativity
- Location: Throat

Dancing with Chakra 5

Dance your fastest, most delicious song and move around the room. If you are chair-bound, not a problem! Engage your upper body and use your vocal cords. Sing your heart out. Express yourself at your wildest. Go for joy!

Chakra 6: Ajna

- Relates to light and inner seeing; represents space, intuition
- Location: The point between the eyebrows at the center of the forehead

Dancing with Chakra 6

This is potentially the sweetest, deepest part of the Let Your Yoga Dance experience. As our energy moves upward to the place between the eyebrows—the third-eye center—we dance away from extroverted wildness and turn our attention inward. We look within to our quiet, intuitive self and with this third, internal-seeking eye, we dance inside ourselves. This part of the class combines dancing yoga cool-down with Dance Prayer. I discovered Dance Prayer over twenty years ago in my own practice. (For more on the sixth chakra and Dance Prayer, see Chapter 6.)

Chakra 7: Sahasrara

- Relates to thought, wisdom, unity
- Location: Crown of the head

Dancing with Chakra 7

Relaxation and meditation bring us to stillness and peace, silent wisdom. We take rest. We feel the lingering effect of the dance of yoga while receiving the brilliance of the body's inner wisdom. In yoga, Savasana, the final resting pose, is said to be the most important posture, as it promotes receptivity and deep relaxation. As dancing yogis take rest on the ground, they receive an opportunity to simply be. Just be. All the chakras, the centers of energy, have been danced and balanced.

LET'S MOVE!
Takeaway 6

Meditation in Motion
Energy Balancer

- Start by taking long, deep nostril breaths for a few moments.
- Stand with your feet hip-width apart. Observe the feet rooted on the Earth, the crown of the head pressing upward toward the sky.
- Feel yourself as a connection between Gaia, Mother Earth, and the vast expanse of sky above you.
- The next time you inhale through the nose, slowly lift the arms out in front of you, to shoulder height. As you exhale, slowly bend the elbows, drawing the arms toward you.
- Bend the knees slightly while slowly lowering the arms back down toward the ground. Press the hands toward the floor in front of you.
- Repeat seven times. Inhaling, let the straight arms rise up in front of the body. Exhaling, bend the knees while drawing the arms toward you and lowering them to the floor.

The slower you go, the more benefits you receive. This promotes a deep sense of relaxation, soothing the mind and calming the nervous system.

CHAPTER 3:

Yamas, Niyamas, and Metta: Loving-Kindness Meditation

The Yamas and Niyamas: Yogic Codes of Conduct

Along with the chakras, Let Your Yoga Dance is also built around ten doctrines that form the foundation of all yoga practice: the yamas and niyamas.

The yamas (mastery and restraint) and niyamas (observances) are values that are woven throughout yogic spiritual practice. Through living and practicing these values, our behavior and our actual thoughts begin to change. The yamas and niyamas are not harsh rules but rather descriptions of human potential. They offer us a way to live in clarity, integrity, and joy. Why joy? Because walking the walk and dancing the dance of ethical behavior leads to congruent living. Congruent living means that one's feelings, thoughts, and actions are in alignment. Anyone exploring Let Your Yoga Dance, as either a teacher or practitioner, learns these essential practices.

Each yama and niyama is like a garland of flowers. When you pick one petal, the entire garland will follow. We cannot practice one yama without picking up the entire garland. By living these codes of conduct to the best of our ability, we access greater energy. Our minds become more focused and flexible. Our energy begins to direct itself internally. As energy rises within, our body and mind become integrated.

Practicing the Yamas and Niyamas

You can become familiar with the yamas and niyamas by picking one and focusing on it each day, each week, or each month. While practicing yoga, Let Your Yoga Dance, and/or meditation, you might repeat the name of that yama or niyama. When a difficult situation arises during the day, recall your practice, using the word as a mantra, inwardly repeating the name over and over. This is not only soothing for the mind, it also sends a new, healthy affirmation into your consciousness.

Yamas and Niyamas, Defined

The Yamas: Mastery, Restraint

Yamas explore our outer environment, the world around us.

Ahimsa: Non-Violence, Compassion

The practice of compassion in action, thought, and speech.

- **Cultivate:** compassion, understanding, patience, self-love, kindness

- **Affirm:** *I do my best to be compassionate in my thinking, my speaking, my doing. When my mind entertains thoughts of fear, anger, or selfishness, I do my best to breathe and relax rather than to act upon these thoughts. As soon as I can, I remember to dance into ahimsa, knowing that the dance will heal me.*

Ahimsa is my go-to yama. When in doubt, I try to be compassionate toward myself and others. When not in doubt, I try to be compassionate toward myself and others. It is common for most teachers and performers to look for what did *not* work in their efforts. Ahimsa looks to strengths. Ahimsa gives us all permission to be human. Following the guidance of ahimsa is a wise choice.

Satya: Truth

The practice of truthfulness of speaking, thinking, or doing.

- **Cultivate:** honesty, owning your feelings, kind communication, assertiveness, giving constructive feedback, forgiveness, non-judgment, letting go of masks

- **Affirm:** *I am a truth-seeker. I live in truth. My body never lies; it speaks the truth. I dance the truth. I speak the truth to myself and to others (when appropriate).*

Satya is a challenging, fascinating practice. I get to ask myself: "When I am lying? Are white lies okay? Am I practicing satya if I hurt someone's feelings? Am I practicing satya if I choose not to speak up? Is it sometimes better—and wiser—to practice the art of not speaking?"

Asteya: Non-Stealing

The practice of not coveting; not being jealous; not stealing time, energy, or the world's resources.

- **Cultivate:** a sense of completeness, self-sufficiency, letting go of cravings

- **Affirm:** *I do my best to be honorable, not stealing time or energy from myself or others. I take and use only what is rightfully mine. I remember that I am enough.*

Asteya helps me with my relationship with Mother Earth. Are my actions stealing from the planet? Can I ride my bike into town today instead of jumping into my car? Can I work harder at being on time to see a friend, colleague, or family member? Instead of coveting someone's talent, can I simply be happy for his or her accomplishment?

Brahmacharya: Moderation, Respect for Energy

The practice of releasing overindulgence of mind, intellect, speech, and body.

- **Cultivate:** moderation on all levels concerning sex, food, work, spiritual practice, the environment, and other aspects of daily life. This is not about repression of sensual cravings; it is about being judicious and gentle with ourselves.

- **Affirm:** *I respect my own energy, and the energy of the world around me. I treat myself and others with respect. When my energy becomes scattered, I come home to my Source and to the primary relationship with myself.*

Brahmacharya is my great teacher. I see Brahmacharya as a practice of self-respect and self-care, with moderation being the key. For decades, before finally letting go of eating sugar and flour, I tried to practice moderation. But then that piece of gooey dessert would stare at me unmercifully—and I'd grab it. Nowadays my moderation struggle leans toward bedtime: I think I am a good dancing yogini, and then I stay up way too late binge-reading my favorite novel. Later I awaken with a start, realizing the book has fallen on my head.

How do I tickle my senses and appreciate the many sensual gifts of being alive, without overdoing? Practicing brahmacharya is like riding a surfboard. When I fall off the board, as I often do, there is always the next moment. I can get back on and surf some more!

Aparigraha: Non-Possessiveness

The practice of fulfilling our needs rather than our wants.

- **Cultivate:** non-attachment to possessions, relationships

- **Affirm:** *I release attachment to other people, to substances, to achieving success in my actions. I recognize the difference between a want and a need. I create inner fulfillment.*

Aparigraha is the yama for teachers. I love this yama! When teaching, I sometimes yearn for the group to "get it," to go with me and be in my space of joy or knowledge. The gentle practice of aparigraha reminds me to let go. It tells me to do my best, rather than cling to a particular outcome. I have practiced this yama on and off for thirty years and still feel like an amateur in this regard. Years ago, one of my students created an aparigraha dance of yoga which I have borrowed ever since. It is a dance of letting go of the fruits of our actions. For me, one of the best ways to practice these yamas and niyamas is to dance them!

Before exploring the niyamas, take a moment to enjoy the seven movements of the spine in a seated position:

LET'S MOVE!
Takeaway 7
Seated Seven Movements of the Spine
Energy Booster

- Begin seated in a chair, with your feet planted firmly on the earth and your hands resting on your thighs.

First and Second Movements: Cat and Dog

- Inhale into Dog by raising the sacrum (lower back) and head slightly upward.

- Exhale into Cat by gently rounding the spine, chin tilting downward. Press your hands into your thighs. Repeat two more times.

Third and Fourth Movements: Half Moon: Lateral Side Flexion, right and left sides

- Inhale, and raise your left arm up as far as is comfortable, lengthening through the spine. Exhale, and arch over to the right side. Left arm can be overhead or it can remain down if necessary. Right elbow can rest on your thigh—or you can bring your right hand to the right ribs and press in and up. This self-assist reminds the torso to lengthen over the ribs, rather than crunching down on them.

- Inhale, and lift back up. Exhale the left arm down.

- Repeat on the other side.

Fifth and Sixth Movements: Rotation, right and left sides

- Inhale, and lengthen the spine; exhale, and gently twist to the right side.
- Inhale; untwist. Exhale; release at center.
- Inhale; lengthen up. Exhale, gently twisting to the left side.
- Inhale; untwist. Exhale, and release.

Seventh Movement: Lengthening the Spine, Seated Mountain Pose (Tadasana)

- Press the sitting bones down into your chair, tailbone dropping down. Simultaneously, press the crown of the head upward without tilting the chin up. Maintain a long, graceful spine.

You have just moved the spine in all the ways it loves to move.

These seven movements can also be done in a standing position or seated on the floor. After you do these movements, your back hopefully will feel better, and you might feel more energized and balanced.

The Niyamas: Observances

The niyamas explore our inner environment.

Saucha: Purity

The practice of cleanliness, good health habits

- **Cultivate:** purity of thought, discrimination. Let Your Yoga Dance is a physical experience of saucha. This form of dancing cleanses not only the physical and mental body, but the emotional body as well.

- **Affirm:** *I cultivate purity in my body by exercising and choosing a wholesome diet. I dance my yoga to purify my body-mind of toxins and mental tensions.*

Saucha is a good friend of mine. I adore swimming, letting my yoga dance, sweating, and feeling physically clean from the inside out. And then I look inside my mind. With what am I filling my mind? Sometimes, in order to practice saucha, I must turn off the computer. Listening to and watching the news can be toxic. With reports happening 24/7 across the globe, it can be completely overwhelming, overstimulating, and frightening to be bombarded with so much information. A lovely practice of saucha is silence. Meditation. A quiet walk in the woods. Swimming in a lake. Walking on a beach. The mind gets to rest and recharge.

Santosha: Contentment

The practice of accepting what is, making the best out of everything

- **Cultivate:** gratitude and joyfulness as a state of mind that does not depend on any external status. If you are performing beneath your standards, remember to be kind to your body, mind, and spirit. When thinking of santosha, bring to mind the face of someone who radiates peace and contentment.

- **Affirm:** *I am content. I am grateful for what I have and for what I do not have. I learn from the joys and disappointments that life brings me. I honor the good in myself and others.*

Dear santosha! This was my very first yoga practice back in 1984. I thought this practice with its velvety name would be easy to follow, but instead I realized in no short order that I was a raging malcontent! Example: When I had lived in the ashram for two years, I was invited by my mentor, Don Stapleton, a tremendously gifted teacher and yogi, to join him and Yogi Amrit Desai on a seminar trip to St Croix. I was beside myself with joy and gratitude. But sixty seconds later, I thought, "Hmmm...will I get to sit next to them on the plane? Or many rows away?" Luckily, I was practicing santosha at the time, so this practice was uppermost in my mind. When I caught myself, I switched gears and chastised my worried mind: "Yo! This trip to St Croix is an honor and a gift. Everyone in the ashram would do anything to go in your place! You be grateful for this wonderful opportunity, Megha, even if you have to ride in the baggage compartment." It worked! I was delighted the entire trip; turns out I was not seated next to Don or the guru on the plane, but I wasn't in the baggage hold either!

Santosha reminds me to be grateful, not only for that which I have, but also for that which I do not have.

Tapas: Discipline

The practice of being willing to do what is necessary to reach a goal. Tapas is a riverbank that keeps the water of your life flowing clear and free.

- **Cultivate:** determination to pursue daily practices, enthusiasm for the spiritual path.

- **Affirm:** *I cultivate discipline. I have strong boundaries and I take good care of myself. I have a realistic, balanced schedule for my work, spiritual practice, and personal needs.*

Tapas separates the dreamers from the doers. Truthfully, I spent fifteen years with this book in my head, dreaming that it would happen. Five years ago, tapas started whispering more and more loudly inside my mind, until it began shouting with a deafening roar: "Do you want this book read by the world? Then get off your feet, sit in a chair (or on the floor), be quiet, and start writing!" And so I did.

Swadhyaya: Self-Study

The practice of expanding knowledge through self-observation.

- **Cultivate:** reading and reflecting, meditation.

- **Affirm:** *I practice conscious awareness throughout the day. I expand my self-knowledge and reflect upon my life with acceptance.*

Swadhyaya has been a consciousness buoy for me. Swami Kripalu taught, "The highest form of spiritual practice is self-observation without judgment." I take time to pause during the day, to ask myself, "What is happening now in my mind? Am I being critical of myself or others? Am I complaining? Am I practicing this niyama well in this moment?" When I carefully, with compassion, look at myself and my thoughts on the Let Your Yoga Dance floor, I am practicing swadhyaya. Research also falls under the category of swadhyaya. Nowadays, I am researching everything I can on Positive Psychology, as well as the art of teaching kids and teens and leading people with special physical and/or emotional needs.

Ishvara-Pranidhana: Letting Go, Surrender to Life

The practice of surrendering. This niyama is in some ways the result of practicing the other nine yamas and niyamas.

- **Cultivate:** dedication, sincerity, and patience to transcend the ego. We need an ego in order to go about our daily lives, but we also need to know when to let go and come into our hearts.

- **Affirm:** *I surrender my ego, my false pride, to life. I release the need for being the doer, no matter whether I fail or succeed in what I do.*

Last but not least: ishvara-pranidhana — the big umbrella over all the other yamas and niyamas. Focusing on ishvara-pranidhana, I ask myself, "What happens when I simply let go and surrender?" This surrender is accomplished through empowerment; it does not mean resignation. Have you heard the saying, "Let go and let God?" Wise counsel. Since September 11, 2001, ishavara-pranidhana has taken on new meaning for me. On that traumatizing day, thousands of people, especially those living in New York City, gave and received open-armed, open-hearted kindness. There was nothing left to do but be kind and compassionate. For a while in New York City, people surrendered to what was, and went into action to serve, to care, to help where they could. Ishvara-pranhidhana is a beautiful, profound practice.

Applied Yamas and Niyamas

During Let Your Yoga Dance teacher training, I introduce the concept of Applied Yamas and Niyamas. I invite the trainees to pick a yama or niyama and play with it for a week, or a month, or perhaps a year. When they lead classes, teachers can frame their class with a particular yama or niyama. For example, if they choose ahimsa (compassionate awareness), they can analyze their class and their performance through the lens of ahimsa. While designing the class, they can ask themselves, "How can ahimsa serve me as I prepare my class, observing the design process before class begins? Are self-judgments coming up for me? Am I being kind to myself?"

While leading the class, they can ask themselves, "How can ahimsa serve me as I teach my Let Your Yoga Dance class? Am I making up stories about my students and their enjoyment—or not—of my class? Am I being critical of myself? Am I losing joy by being self-concerned instead of giving more care to my students?" It is quite possible to use ahimsa as a self-soothing opportunity.

When the class is over, teachers can recapitulate: "How can ahimsa serve me now that the class is over? Did I enjoy the class? What went well? Was I compassionate and kind with myself as well as my students?" If the class did not go as well as I hoped, I can use ahimsa to be compassionate with myself. "Did I do my best? Can I learn something from this class to try the next time?" Compassionate awareness is simply profound.

I have found that the Applied Yamas and Niyamas are important yogic guides; they ground me in the foundational practices of yoga as I bring Let Your Yoga Dance to students around the world.

The yamas and niyamas have been practiced for thousands of years. They have been a great anchor, ally, and friend to me for many decades, and a core value for Let Your Yoga Dance. Consider delving into a yama or niyama and see what happens.

LET'S MOVE!
Takeaway 8

Do-In: A Japanese Form of Self-Massage
Energy Booster

Do-In (pronounced "Dough-Eeeen") is a form of self-massage. It's a great way to honor the body, and a wonderful boost when you are tired. Before you begin, feel free to play a song from any genre that makes you smile or laugh.

- Start by shaking out your hands until they tingle with energy.

- Begin to tap the crown of the head with the tips of your fingers. Move your way down the skull; then tap the forehead, temples, and the whole terrain of your face. Tap your throat, neck, and then your shoulders.

- Moving down the body, make loose fists, and begin to pound them into your chest. Turn your tap into a pummel.

- Make a Tarzan sound: "AAAHHH." Begin to pummel the top of your right arm with your left fist, from the shoulder down to your hand, then up the underside. Keep breathing deeply. Now pummel across your chest again, then move to the top of the left arm. Pummel down to the hand, and back up the underside of the left arm.

- Now, with your fists, pummel all the way down the top of your right leg. First pummel down the front of the leg, then back up the underside. When ready, switch to the left leg.

- Create a balancing pose by lifting your right bent leg. If you can reach your right foot, slap the top and bottom of the foot simultaneously, as if giving it a well deserved round of applause. Don't forget the left side! This stimulates all the nerve endings in your feet.

While in a meeting, reading, traveling, keep checking in with the body. Move, wiggle, stretch as much as you like. The research has been out for years, telling us no matter what age we are:

Move it or lose it.

Metta, the Practice of Loving-Kindness

Along with the yamas and niyamas, there is another important spiritual practice inherent to Let Your Yoga Dance: the ancient Buddhist practice of metta, or loving-kindness. Metta is a friendliness practice; its benefits can be instantaneous. With practice, it cultivates kind mental states of benevolence and goodwill. Metta melts down the barriers that cause separation, counteracting and disarming the judging mind. Over time, as we send loving-kindness unto others, we, too, become happier.

Practicing Metta

Start by sending metta to yourself. You can do so by reciting the following: "May I be happy. May I know peace. May I be free."

Then send metta to a benefactor, spiritual teacher, or mentor.

Next, send metta to a dear friend or significant other.

If possible, send metta to a difficult person. At first, start with an "easy" difficult person, someone for whom you only have a slight aversion. Save the "difficult" difficult person for later, when you feel more solid in the practice. If you simply cannot send metta to this person, then return to yourself.

Lastly, send metta to all beings.

Applied Metta Through Let Your Yoga Dance

You can send Applied Metta to yourself and the world. Start with a simple recitation, repeating "May you be happy, as I wish to be happy, may you be peaceful, as I wish to be peaceful." Later, consider taking the practice into the body: getting up, breathing deeply, and stepping one leg forward into Warrior pose. As you extend your arms overhead, picture your loved ones and all beings.

My teacher, Sylvia Boorstein, mentions loving-kindness in all her books. In *Pay Attention for Goodness Sake*, she shares that loving-kindness meditation helps to focus the mind through wishing others well—a practice of benevolence. In August 2003, during her meditation retreat at Kripalu, I was touched by Sylvia's heartfelt dedication to metta practice, and her reminder that metta is an inner, rather than external, exploration of love.

Although there are hundreds of metta resolves, Sylvia's version is particularly meaningful to me:

> **May all beings be protected and safe.**
>
> **May all beings feel contented and pleased.**
>
> **May all physical bodies be supported with strength.**
>
> **May all lives unfold smoothly with ease.**

With Sylvia's permission, I rearranged the third line of her metta prayer (which, by the way, is a limerick—she loves limericks!) to suit my needs, as follows:

> **May we be protected and safe.**
>
> **May we feel contented and pleased.**
>
> **May our body-mind-spirit be lifted in grace.**
>
> **May our lives unfold smoothly with ease.**

These metta resolves deepen the experience of Let Your Yoga Dance. The benefits of teaching, sharing, and leading metta are almost instantaneous.

LET'S MOVE!
Takeaway 9

Applied Moving Metta
Energy Balancer

The practice of metta is love in action. When dancing in a group, the energy can shift quickly to a calm, sweet state. In fact, it is delightful to experience "moving metta" by offering these resolves to one another as we let our yoga dance together! You can do it right now, even when you're practicing alone; imagine that the whole world is with you.

- Come to standing, or stay seated if need be. Imagine that you're in a room full of people, even if you are alone. Enter into Crane pose, Balakikasana, by shifting your weight onto your left leg and slowly lifting your bent right knee in front of you, no higher than hip height. Simultaneously, stretch out your arms to the sides at shoulder height.

- Now step forward with your right foot, extending your arms forward, as if you were reaching toward a dear friend. Your legs are in a gentle Warrior pose, right leg bent, left leg straight. Imagine looking at a loved one as you say inwardly, "May you be happy, as I wish to be happy." When repeating, "As I wish to be happy," lean back on your left leg, and bring your hands to your heart. You are offering metta first to another; then you offer the metta prayer to yourself.

- Now repeat the next line: "May you be peaceful, as I wish to be peaceful."

- Lean forward as you offer metta; lean back as you offer it to yourself. "May you have ease, as I wish to have ease." "May you be free, as I wish to be free." Repeat the phrases, beginning to think of all beings on earth as you do so.

- Switch to the other leg and repeat the sequence.

Moving metta with your body is powerful medicine.

CHAPTER 4

Positive Psychology and Let Your Yoga Dance

What is meaningful to me?
What brings me pleasure?
What are my deepest strengths?

My History with Positive Psychology

In 2011, as I was leading my Let Your Yoga Dance Teacher Training at Kripalu, a spry, energetic fellow with glasses and a bit of a serious demeanor would occasionally show up to my noon classes. He would often speak with me after class; once he even asked if I would like to bring my training to Israel. "Sure," I said. "I have a simple business plan: I go where I'm asked." Soon, in the hallways of Kripalu, people would say to me, "Tal really likes you!" Whoever this Tal was, I was happy he enjoyed my classes. The next thing I knew, Tal became my trainee in Module 1 of Let Your Yoga Dance Teacher Training. At the end, he gave me a gift, his book *Being Happy*.

Months later, I noticed a huge poster at Kripalu advertising the Certificate in Positive Psychology (CiPP) program, an eleven-month online certification in Positive Psychology that included two on-site immersions at Kripalu. It was to be led by none other than Tal Ben-Shahar, my student! Though not exactly sure what Positive Psychology was, I had an immediate inspiration: Because Let Your Yoga Dance is founded in joy, I felt that Tal's program could use a jolt of Let Your Yoga Dance during the on-site immersions. I sent Tal an e-mail suggesting that I bring Let Your Yoga Dance to the mix.

Due to his evidence and research-based teachings, Tal was not quite sold at first, but I finally convinced him. I told him I was going to focus on the teaching tenets he planned to offer: things like gratitude, resilience, zest, and love. I was going to create for him an Expanding Joy embodied movement curriculum. That sealed the deal. So I became a CiPP faculty member, and Let Your Yoga Dance for Positive Psychology was born.

Before I led my first class during CiPP, Tal came over to me and whispered, "Megha, do you think our 190 trainees can get out of their comfort zone enough to do this? They're not your typical students."

"Tal, I think we'll be fine," I replied, hopefully.

In no time, we were all whooping, singing, and dancing our way around Kripalu's Main Hall. It was wonderful.

In the ensuing years, Let Your Yoga Dance has indeed helped CiPP participants embody the teachings of Positive Psychology. In fact, some CiPP graduates have gone on to become Let Your Yoga Dance instructors!

What Is Positive Psychology?

In that first year of CiPP, while teaching Tal's students, I was simultaneously discovering what Positive Psychology actually was, and what Positive Psychology and Let Your Yoga Dance had in common.

Positive Psychology is the science of happiness. I believe it is also the science of resilience. Positive Psychology dates back to Socrates, Aristotle, and, later, to Abraham Maslow, whose 1954 book *Motivation and Personality* includes a chapter titled "Toward a Positive Psychology." Instead of asking, as many therapists do when starting out with a new client, "What's wrong?", Positive Psychology begins by asking, "What's right?" It explores these important questions:

What is meaningful to me? What brings me pleasure?
What are my deepest strengths?

Positive Psychology doesn't pretend that trauma, grief, clinical depression, and deep sorrow do not exist. It simply wants us to remember that joy, optimism, courage, zest, and resilience exist as well. Positive Psychology is a well-researched science that explores the possibility of thriving and flourishing, no matter what the circumstances.

The person who really put Positive Psychology on the map was Dr. Martin Seligman. A professor at the University of Pennsylvania for more than forty years, Seligman has written hundreds of articles and books on Positive Psychology, including his book *Flourish*. He also gave a Ted Talk that succinctly explains Positive Psychology.

Seligman has worked with the United States Army, teaching the military about post-traumatic growth (PTG). Most of us have heard of post-traumatic stress disorder, but fewer people know about PTG. Having witnessed the plethora of psychologically wounded and traumatized warriors returning from Iraq and Afghanistan, Seligman believes it is possible to create a military that is just as psychology healthy as it is physically fit. (For more information, read *Harvard Business Review*, April 2011, "Post-Traumatic Growth and Building Resilience," and a *New York Times* article from March 22, 2012: "Post-Traumatic Stress's Surprisingly Positive Flip Side," by Jim Rendonmarch.)

Although research is not yet conclusive, it certainly appears that if veterans, who have stared death in the face in the worst possible conditions, can experience post-traumatic growth—and many can and do—then hopefully all of us can.

LET'S MOVE!
Takeaway 10
Helicopter Rotations with Ha Breaths
Energy Booster

Do you remember the LET'S MOVE! Takeaway 7: The Seven Movements of the Spine? This upcoming helicopter sequence rotates the spine from right to left, using the fifth and sixth movements of the spine.

If you are new to the movement world, or have spinal issues, check in with your doctor before trying this, as it involves twisting the spine rapidly. For some folks, spinal rotation is contraindicated, especially if there is hardware in your spine.

- Come to a standing position to enter the yoga pose Five-Pointed Star. Legs are wide apart, arms outstretched at shoulder height.

- Take three long, deep breaths.

- Now drop your arms, turning them into "empty coat sleeves." Start to flap them around your body, rotating from side to side. Start slowly.

The faster you go, the more heat you will build in the body. Hot-flashing women, beware: These helicopter movements will indeed warm you up, easily inducing a hot flash. If you want to stay cool, slow down! A slow-moving helicopter is fine, too!

- Rotate with the helicopter for forty-five seconds. You might, if you're lucky, get a free chiropractic adjustment while you're at it!

Discovering our Strengths with Positive Psychology

VIA: Values in Action

Values in Action (VIA) was co-created by Martin Seligman and the late Chris Peterson, who was a professor at the University of Michigan. VIA is a fascinating inquiry into your own strengths. Seligman and Peterson created a list of twenty-four character strengths that reach beyond age, social status, gender, and nationality. These character strengths include such Positive Psychology stalwarts as gratitude, generosity, resilience, love, enthusiasm, and optimism.

VIA Strengths:

To take the free twenty-minute test and find your top strengths, visit viacharacter.org

I have learned through VIA that my top strengths are gifts that I don't have to struggle to attain; they are my signature strengths. My top four strengths are gratitude, love, appreciation of beauty and excellence, and humor. Who knew? I was relieved to learn that the lowest-ranking VIA strengths on your list can, over time, be pushed up to a higher level.

This test has been taken by millions of people around the world. Go online and take the free questionnaire to find out your top character strengths. It's fun, interesting, and enlightening. There is even a VIA questionnaire for teens!

Wholebeing and Deeper Meaning

I am grateful for Tal's extensive study into the science of happiness. Tal pulls together the Positive Psychology research and disseminates it in a way that allows people the world over, not only academics, to understand it. He then invites us to use the information in our own lives, and then to spread it, to serve it forward.

Tal has a concise definition of happiness: pleasure with deeper meaning. Tal, along with my friend and colleague, Megan McDonough, a corporate trainer, author, and yoga teacher, coined the term "wholebeing," which is also the name of the institute that he and Megan cofounded. Wholebeing encompasses the many facets that make up a human being: body, heart, mind/intellect, spirit,

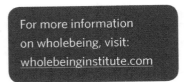
For more information
on wholebeing, visit:
wholebeinginstitute.com

dark/light, fear, resilience, joy, and sorrow. Wholebeing brings pleasure with deeper meaning to our lives. I know that, for me, when nothing is excluded from my psyche, I am, indeed, happier.

Abraham Maslow's Contribution to Positive Psychology

At the beginning of this chapter, I mentioned Abraham Maslow, a pioneer in the fields of humanistic and transpersonal psychology. Today, he is considered by many to be the Grandfather of Positive Psychology.

Maslow's "hierarchy of needs triangle" was first proposed in a paper he wrote in 1943 called "A Theory of Human Motivation."

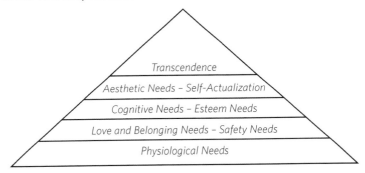

Writer, psychodramatist, and Positive Psychologist Dan Tomasulo, who assists Dr. Seligman in the University of Pennsylvania's Master of Arts degree program in Positive Psychology, wrote to me a few years back about the similarities he'd noticed between the Hierarchy of Needs and the chakra system. He shared with me his 2011 article in Psych Central entitled, "Hierarchy of Chakras?" in which he wrote:

> Deficiency motivation vs. growth motivation is at the essence of Maslow's hierarchy of needs. You've seen the pyramid. It would be hard to find an introductory psychology book that doesn't have this neatly layered and colored design. These color schemes follow a familiar pattern: Red, orange-yellow, green-blue; blue-purple; violet. Of course it is the color spectrum, but it is interesting to see the same down-up coloring of the 7 chakras. But the alignment between Maslow's hierarchy and the correlation to the chakras may not be so farfetched.

Decide for yourself if Maslow's theory may have had earlier roots in the "powerhouse of the Universe." Here is a direct comparison of Maslow's hierarchy of needs and the 7 chakras.

Maslow's Hierarchy of Needs	Chakras
Self-Actualization (morality, creativity, spontaneity, problem-solving, lack of prejudice, and acceptance of facts)	**Seventh Chakra:** understanding, self-knowledge, and higher consciousness **Sixth Chakra:** Imagination, awareness, self-reflection, and intuition **Fifth Chakra:** self-expression, and deeper connection to others
Esteem (confidence, achievement, respect of others, and respect by others)	**Fourth Chakra:** love, self-acceptance, balanced perspective, and compassion
Love and Belongingness (family, friendship, and sexual intimacy)	**Third Chakra:** esteem, power and position, strength, and status
Safety and Security (of body, resources, family, health, employment, and property)	**Second Chakra:** order, love, and belonging
Physiological Needs (breathing, food, water, air, sex, sleep, homeostasis, and excretion)	**First Chakra:** Life, survival, and safety

Because Let Your Yoga Dance is based on the chakras, I was both fascinated and delighted to observe these two models placed side by side. Tomasulo went on to write:

> Whether knowing of the chakras influenced Maslow's thinking or not, in the end both point to human beings striving for higher levels of creativity, health and self-fulfillment. Blocks at lower levels impede this growth, and the tendency toward this higher level is natural, even essential.

Although the chakras have yet to make their way into the scientific research lexicon, that does not mean they have no value. They're just way ahead of their time! In yogic anatomy, the body's energy centers have been studied and honored for thousands of years.

LET'S MOVE!
Takeaway 11

Synovial Shake
Energy Booster

This next takeaway is fun! Feel free to put some upbeat music on for this lively shake out. Synovial fluid bathes and lubricates all the joints in the body. This exercise is especially important for anyone older than 40; with age, it becomes more difficult for synovial fluid to reach the joints, so the occasional shake can be most beneficial.

You can do this practice either standing or sitting, but if you are able to stand, do. You will receive a bonus of balancing.

- Start by shaking your fingers as fast as you comfortably can, awakening your knuckle joints.

- Now move on to the wrists, shaking them out, too. Then the elbows. Then the shoulders.

- Now shake the fingers, wrists, elbows, and shoulders all at the same time. As you continue shaking, start to wiggle all the joints in your spine.

- Shake from the cervical vertebrae in the neck all the way down to the sacral and coccyx vertebrae at the base of the spine.

- Keep all those joints moving while you pick up your right foot and shake out the right hip, then the right knee, the right ankle, and the right toes.

- Now repeat on the left side: Hip, knee, ankle, toes.

- Now just shake everything out—go wild and free!

Positive Paradigms

The more I learn about Positive Psychology, the happier I become. It validates so much of my own worldview. Bringing the body into Positive Psychology has given me tremendous pleasure. I have created a new branch of Let Your Yoga Dance for the Positive Psychology world. For decades, I couldn't understand why the body had been overlooked in our culture's more traditional psychological fields. Fortunately, things are beginning to change and evolve. The body is receiving newfound respect in Western culture. Hallelujah!

Some elementary schools now have stationary bikes in the classroom so that kids can exercise while studying, rather than trying to sit still hour after hour. The North American culture still has a long way to go in respecting the body, but changes are happening, slowly and surely.

Introverts, Extroverts, and Ambiverts Dancing Their Yoga

Our Certificate in Positive Psychology (CiPP) program attracts all kinds of personalities. We begin our eleven-month course by observing introversion and extroversion. Although labeling personalities can be somewhat tricky, exploring introverted and extroverted qualities in oneself and others can be beneficial.

Sue Cain's lovely book *Quiet* offers an insightful look at introversion in our Western culture, and the difficulties many introverts endure. This was helpful for me to read because I have found that some introverts, though not all, tend to avoid Let Your Yoga Dance. They might feel shy or perhaps overstimulated by this ebullient practice.

I learned an unfamiliar term in Cain's book: ambivert. An ambivert is someone who is equally introverted and extroverted. Having lived in a highly extroverted world for decades, teaching and training thousands of people a year, and being an actor before that, I would race home after work and collapse into a lavender-scented bubble bath with candles flickering on the windowsill. I never answered my phone. I rarely wanted to go to parties. (And I still don't!)

When I heard the term ambivert, I thought I must be an ambivert as well. But actually, with further study, and from hearing Tal's way of determining where you fall on the spectrum (he recommends asking yourself, "Do you have a bunch of friends or just a handful?"), I have bowed to the inevitable: I am a tried and true extrovert who also needs a lot of down time! Though I continue to seek quiet anywhere I can, it turns out that I'm just trying to rebalance myself after a busy day of teaching in CiPP or my Let Your Yoga Dance Teacher Training.

Many people throughout the years have stood in the doorway of my classes, gazing at the exuberant people dancing their yoga with abandon. Sometimes they have said something like "I am an introvert. I am more comfortable curled up with a book and a cup of tea. This Let Your Yoga Dance thing is way out of my comfort zone."

I have come to realize that if I can just woo them into the Let Your Yoga Dance studio for five or ten minutes, they might just get hooked! Suddenly what was not their comfort zone becomes their comfort zone. A student of mine, Ruth Pearce, explains her experience as a self-professed introvert who loves Let Your Yoga Dance. She writes:

> One of the pleasures of the Certificate in Positive Psychology (CiPP) program is that it is not all in our heads. At the CiPP immersion, the beauty and accessibility of Let Your Yoga Dance for Positive Psychology was a revelation to me. While many people are surprised to learn that I am an introvert—one who has managed to learn to "fake it 'til I make it"—it is nonetheless true. Before CiPP, the thought of being in a room of people, getting my groove on, would have made me melt into a puddle of butter! Enter Megha. At the start of class, she pointed around the room and told us: "You are all dancers." "Yeah, right," I thought, "You haven't seen me yet!"

> Fifteen minutes in, I had lost ALL inhibition and was dancing and moving, pulling Lion's Breath faces, dancing my Mountain Pose and Warrior along with everyone else. I felt light, at ease, and completely unconcerned with my inhibitions and other peoples' opinions.

> The result has been profound. In recent times, I have been seen dancing in the strangest places—cemeteries, under the trees near the Normal Rockwell Museum, and on my lawn across from the golf club. Time stops, I am in flow, I lose all sense of myself. I forget myself. Although, on the outside, I look extroverted, I am actually totally introverted and introspective, reveling in my own well-being.

Other Let Your Yoga Dance class members have described the same experience. Many people who hover on the sidelines, too reserved and nervous at first to come in, try the five-minute ramp-up and, before they have time to give nervousness another thought, they are hooked!

Who could fail to be an avid enthusiast of a form of dancing yoga where you do abdominal work and don't notice, because you are too busy sending well wishes to people in the room? Everyone in the class feels special. Every person in the room IS special! We are focused not on exercise but on community. We can sweat with abandon along with 50+ of our closest family members—because we are all family members in that moment.

CiPP Australia

Speaking of introverts getting hooked, I am smiling now as I think with delight about my new students and friends in Australia. In July 2015, we took CiPP Down Under to the Geelong Grammar School, near Melbourne. Folks from all over Australia, New Zealand, Japan, Vietnam, and Taiwan registered. Many were nonplussed about the idea of letting their yoga dance. Many of them cried out, "I am a dyed-in-the-wool introvert! This will be way too far from my comfort zone!" But they decided to stick around and see what would happen if they let their yoga dance. Within seconds, just as people do everywhere else in the world, they were whooping, hooting, and laughing!

Positive Education at the Geelong Grammar School

An interesting aside: Our CiPP course in Australia is housed at the Geelong Grammar School, a middle and high school for both day students and boarders. This special school is dedicated to the teachings of Positive Psychology, which school leaders have renamed Positive Education.

Years ago, Martin Seligman and his colleagues from the University of Pennsylvania spent time at the school, training not only administrators, teachers, and students, but also cooks, cleaners, janitorial workers, and parents. The intention was to bring the entire school community into the mix so that all of Geelong would subsequently understand and implement the teaching tenets of Positive Education. A great book, *Positive Education*, has been written by Jacolyn Norrish, with the help of Geelong Grammar School faculty and administrators.

LET'S MOVE!
Takeaway 12
Breath of Fire Energy Booster
Energy Booster

Breath of Fire is a great way to increase your energy level. This is done either seated or standing, making short, rapid expulsions of breath through the nostrils. The impetus is all from the belly. It's rapid sniffing, both inhaling and exhaling. If you have any blood pressure issues, take long, slow deep breaths instead. Feel free to play some upbeat music if you like.

- With tall, erect spine, inhale through the nostrils. Then, forcefully pull the belly in as you exhale—once again through the nostrils.

- Repeat, gradually increasing your tempo. If you are new to the practice, explore the Breath of Fire for about thirty seconds. Over time, you may increase to one minute.

This is a powerful builder of energy in the body. If you feel lightheaded during the practice, stop and return to slow, deep breaths.

CHAPTER 5:

The SPIRE Model
of
Whole-Person Well-Being

S	P	I	R	E
SPIRITUAL	PHYSICAL	INTELLECTUAL	RELATIONAL	EMOTIONAL
Focusing on purpose and meaning. Knowing the values that drive your actions.	Cultivating positive regard for your body. Being aware of its ability to affect mind.	Stretching the mind by cultivating creativity and a love of learning.	Contributing to and benefiting from community. Nurturing a relationship with self.	Reinforcing affirming emotions. Cultivating resilience to manage painful emotions.

Moving Toward a Happier, More Authentic Life

Our world is filled with diagrams, anagrams, and roadmaps to help us find our way to the most congruent life imaginable. Having read thus far, you know that my primary consciousness tools, along with Let Your Yoga Dance itself, are the yamas and niyamas, moving yoga, mindful meditation, the chakra system, and metta practice. I have studied and taught these roadmaps for thirty years; they work. Therefore, it is a testimony to the Wholebeing Institute co-founders, Tal Ben-Shahar and Megan McDonough, that I have also heartily embraced their SPIRE model of whole-person well-being. SPIRE is an acronym they created, which stands for:

Spiritual, Physical, Intellectual, Relational, and Emotional.

The breakdown of the anagram looks like this:

S – Spiritual

Focusing on purpose and meaning.
Knowing the values that drive your actions.

P - Physical

Cultivating positive regard for your body.
Being aware of its ability to affect the mind.

I - Intellectual

Stretching the mind by cultivating creativity and a love of learning.

R - Relational

Contributing to and benefiting from community.
Nurturing a relationship with self.

E - Emotional

Reinforcing affirming emotions.
Cultivating resilience to manage painful emotions.

When you join these five letters—S, P, I, R, and E—an inspiring map to health and wholebeing is created. These elements, when explored together, pave the way to a more authentic, joyous life. I have been studying the SPIRE model as a pathway to consciousness, just as I have with the chakras. I consider both to be solid ground upon which we can dance through our lives with pleasure and deeper meaning.

SPIRE is a great gift to the world of Positive Psychology in particular and psychology in general, because it embraces the physical: the body. The "talking cure" has often neglected the body, focusing primarily on the mind as the way toward healing.

For me, SPIRE is like wrapping paper. When I wrap SPIRE around my choices, I get a gift: My life becomes more well-rounded, more mindful, and happier. With SPIRE, I can observe the present moment and my next steps from a spiritual and physical perspective, an intellectual perspective, and a relational and emotional perspective. In this way, I've got my bases covered.

SPIRE teaches that our bodies, minds, and hearts need to be cherished and used with both rigor and care. We have intellects; we have kinesthetically curious brains. That curiosity can be about any topic that inspires us to dive deeply into study. SPIRE also reminds us that we are relational beings. Even if we are embarking on a solo journey, there are often others helping us (sometimes invisibly) along the way. For example, Henry David Thoreau could not have succeeded with his log cabin experiment at Walden Pond had his loving mother and sister not made themselves available to bring him food and do his laundry!

SPIRE
and the Yogic Koshas

Because much of my life has been dedicated to yoga and letting my yoga dance, I feel that one more diagram is in order to complete the tapestry of the chakras in Let Your Yoga Dance and the SPIRE model in Positive Psychology.

For thousands of years, ancient yogic science has demonstrated that human beings are multidimensional. In yogic anatomy, it is said that five layers, or sheaths of existence, reside within us. These layers are called the koshas. In my view, they blend quite nicely with SPIRE.

The first layer, or sheath, is the physical body, known as the Anamaya Kosha. This first sheath intersects with the P, the physical aspect, of SPIRE.

The second layer is the breath or energy sheath, known as the Pranamaya Kosha. To me, this layer relates to S, the spiritual aspect, of SPIRE. The breath (from the Latin: *inspire*) joins us every step of the way, throughout our lives. Whenever we are in trouble, stress, doubt, or fear, the antidote is simple: Breathe. With breath, we connect with something deeper: the mystery of life itself.

The third sheath is the mind-emotional layer of the self: the Manomaya Kosha, which walks hand-in-hand with E, the emotional aspect of SPIRE. With this embrace of emotions, we discover ourselves to be resourceful and resilient.

The fourth layer is the witness, the part of our self that discerns and watches with dispassionate, compassionate awareness: the Vijnanamaya Kosha. One might think of this layer as "the still, small voice within." I actually think it is a loud, flowing voice within, but our lives can be so stressful that we become deaf to its persistent call. It is hard to hear the Vijnanamaya Kosha when we are so distracted by the demanding culture in which we live. I think of this kosha as the higher mind; it ties in with I, the intellectual aspect, of SPIRE.

Last but not least, the fifth layer of the self is the Anandamaya Kosha. *Ananda* means "bliss." I feel comforted to know that we humans house a layer devoted to joy, bliss, and rapture. Our birthright, from the yogic perspective, is to experience a deep, internal relationship with bliss. In SPIRE, the Relational – R – aspect, is not only about relating with others; it is also about the relationship we have with ourselves.

Choosing Joy

What is our relationship with bliss and joy? That's a question for a whole other book. It seems to me that our overmedicated culture runs far away from our birthright of bliss. We do what we can to overcome depression, but don't we also tamp down our bliss? Do we know how to contain that much joy? Is it safe to feel that much joy? I like to think I have a great capacity for joy; I was lucky enough to be born with cheerful genes and two great parents who loved me. However, it is still too easy a habit, even for someone as fortunate as I have been, to grab too much comfort food when I'm feeling overly glad, mad, sad, or scared! Many of us were not instructed as children to discover all the ways in which we could increase our tolerance for joy. Is it possible to simply choose joy and learn to just be with it when it graces us with its presence? That's where the inSPIREd dance of yoga comes in!

InSPIREd Let Your Yoga Dance

As I said previously, since SPIRE entered my life, I have begun to look at my choices from the SPIRE perspective, along with the lens of the chakras. Using the anagram, I'll demonstrate how I blend SPIRE and the chakras in Let Your Yoga Dance. For me, this is a yellow brick road leading to expanded joy and deeper consciousness.

The Spiritual in SPIRE

In the spiritual aspect of SPIRE, gratitude is a key component. Let Your Yoga Dance is filled with dances of gratitude—gratitude to the body, to loved ones, and to the larger community. These gratitude dances appear most prevalently in the fourth (heart) and sixth (intuitive) chakras. Presence and mindfulness are also key elements in the spiritual aspect of SPIRE. We leap into the present moment—into spirit—when we let our yoga dance.

Music for S in SPIRE

Karen Drucker, "Thank You for this Day"

Sinead O'Connor, "Thank You"

Linda Worster, "One Word"

The Physical in SPIRE

SPIRE welcomes the body into the realm of psychology. The P can take the form of any type of exercise: Let Your Yoga Dance, qi gong, yoga, running, hula-hooping, all sports. Just because I love to dance my yoga does not mean this must be your physical choice. One of my amusing colleagues tells her students: "I'm not into yoga; I'll take a bat and a ball anytime!" One special plus in SPIRE's relationship with Let Your Yoga Dance is the strong aerobic component of the practice. Students receive an aerobic workout without knowing it! They are so busy focusing on qualities like love, gratitude, resilience, and positivity that it is often only at the end of class, when folks are sweaty and wrung out, that they realize they have not only experienced a great play-in, but a work-out as well! During class, the breath deepens, which helps to build lung capacity. As the heart starts pumping, sweat pours out, joy builds, and happy hormones are released. Students forget to be self-conscious, and instead enter into a blissful state of flow.

Music for P in SPIRE

will.i.am.,
"Different Strokes for Different Folks"

Pharrel Williams,
"Happy"

Destiny's Child,
"Bootylicious"

The Intellectual in SPIRE

The intellectual component of SPIRE is about deep study—both within and without—and also about fostering creativity and witness. The I also relates to Brain Health in Let Your Yoga Dance. For me, it is very important to teach some new steps in every class so that the hippocampus keeps firing, which, in turn, helps dancers' brains to stay sharp. Learning dance steps and dancing yoga movements can create new neural pathways, which then teach the body to move in more intuitive, organic ways, along with keeping the brain healthy and smart.

Music for I in SPIRE

Stevin McNamara,
"Moon Magic"

MC Yogi,
"Be the Change"

John de Kadt,
"Three Worlds"

Eva Cassidy,
"Imagine"

The Relational in SPIRE

The R of SPIRE is about connection—with self, others, and the world community. The fourth chakra, the energy center relating to the heart center, merges beautifully with this relational aspect. In Let Your Yoga Dance, we build heart health by simultaneously fostering a compassionate relationship with the group, as well as a kinder, deeper relationship with the self. Our Let Your Yoga Dance mantra, "I've got your back," is a cornerstone of the practice. We dance into relationship with one another. Let Your Yoga Dance builds community through eye contact, partnering, circle dances, and heartfelt music in a safe, fun environment.

Music for R in SPIRE

Bruno Mars,
"Just the Way You Are"

Tina Malia,
"Heal This Land"

Chris Tomlin,
"There is Love"

Pink,
"Just Give Me a Reason"

The Emotional in SPIRE

Our human container is filled with every possible emotion. The E in SPIRE reminds us that all emotions are welcome, be they joyous or difficult. Resilience itself is a big part of the E. With resilience, we can pick ourselves up like the phoenix rising from the ashes. It takes a lot of courage to be a human phoenix, staring our challenging emotions in the face. Remember: It always helps to breathe, breathe, and breathe again. We can also feel, observe, and let the emotions to be just as they are—without fearing them or trying to push them away.

Music for E in SPIRE

Wade Imre Moresette,
"Bala"

Linda Worster,
"Lullabye"

Christina Perry,
"A Thousand Years"

Josh Groban,
"You Raise Me Up"

Doing this helps us to gather our courage, to notice and name emotional difficulties as they arise. "What am I feeling right now" is an excellent question. It brings us to the present and helps us discover what the heart is trying to say.

In Let Your Yoga Dance, when we dance with powerful rhythms and with words like "what doesn't kill you makes you stronger" or "thank you for this day, spirit, thank you for this day," we build resilience kinesthetically and emotionally. The use of upbeat or poignant music taps into our emotions and can dramatically improve mood. The motion in Let Your Yoga Dance creates e-motion, as opposed to the way we usually function, with the mind creating emotion. The evocative dance prayer section can have a powerful effect on participants' emotional well-being.

Appreciative Inquiry

Another way to tap into emotional well-being is through Appreciative Inquiry. David Cooperrider, Professor of the Department of Organizational Behavior at Case Western Reserve University, has done pioneering work in Appreciative Inquiry, introducing it to individuals, businesses, and organizations around the world. In a nutshell, Appreciative Inquiry is defined as looking to the strengths of your past, pulling those strengths into the present, then envisioning those strengths to build yourself a powerful future.

Due to its focus on strengths, Appreciative Inquiry ties in beautifully with my strength-based model in Let Your Yoga Dance Teacher Training.

I would like to experiment now with bringing Appreciative Inquiry together with SPIRE to glean strengths from my choices in the past to see how they have informed my present, and will continue to build a strong future.

Looking Back: How SPIRE Worked for Me

Earlier in the book, I told you a story about a choice I made in 1984 that turned my life in a completely different direction. I put my acting career in New York City on hold and moved to Kripalu for the month of August to become a Spiritual Lifestyle Trainee. That month became twelve years. Thirty years later, my life continues to be impacted by that small yet momentous choice. Throughout the decades, I have continued to do the work I learned and created while living the life of an ashram resident. Using Appreciative Inquiry, what were some strengths I brought to the ashram table? I brought my energy, my dance, my years as a Shakespearean actress, my love of spirituality, and my teaching ability. Using the strengths I showed up with, what happened during those twelve years? Well, I became an expert in experiential education. I delved deeply into the mystery of yoga, which I then brought to my already established dance practice. I became a teacher-trainer at Kripalu. And as I trained others in this work, I became determined to give my trainees a kind, compassionate learning environment. As I observe the present, I see, with Appreciative Inquiry, that my thirty-day choice in 1984 informed my life into the twenty first century. As I look to the future, I only want to bring these teachings and strengths further outward through the world.

But what, you might be asking, has this got to do with SPIRE? A lot! SPIRE did not even exist as a concept back then, but, with hindsight, it is clear that I was integrating those five in-SPIRE-ing elements into my life. I was constantly evaluating and reevaluating my choice. I kept choosing to stay at the ashram, because my connection to my first love, theater, was dwindling.

Why did I stay at Kripalu? Because I felt *spiritually* compelled to remain there. I was in the midst of a unique, noble, spiritual experiment in living. *Physically*, I thrived. We practiced yoga. I danced. We ate organic food. We lived in a holistic health center. *Intellectually*, I was on a huge learning curve. Holistic teachers, such as Deepak Chopra, Ann Wigmore (the creator of Living Foods), and Swami Satchidananda (the "Woodstock" guru) visited and taught the Kripalu residents. Deepak came to us long before he was a household name. During those years of constant learning and inspiration, I was in awe much of the time.

Relationally, I was taught to communicate in new ways. As a community, we were taught to love ourselves, one another, and the thousands of guests that walked through our doors each year. As I began to teach at Kripalu, I often used the words of Kripalu's founder, Amrit Desai: "I haven't come to teach you, but to love you, and the love alone will teach you." I took that phrase as my own. I use it to this day with my students and trainees.

Emotionally, during the ashram era, I kept asking myself, "How does my heart feel about staying here? Is my heart okay with this choice? How do I feel?" And the answer from that not-so-still, not-so-small voice inside my heart was always the same: "Yup–hang in there. You're in the right place." My heart was strong. It knew my choice was the right one. So I stayed put.

I have just given you a personal example of Appreciative Inquiry and making a choice using SPIRE. Why don't you give it a try?

AWARENESS PAUSE
Takeaway 13

Making an inSPIREd Choice
Awareness Pause

- Take a moment to pause. Begin to take some long, deep breaths, inhaling and exhaling.

- The next time you inhale, tilt your head gently upward. On the exhale, tilt your head down.

- Inhale, bring your head back to center. Exhale, turn your head slowly to the right.

- Inhale, return the head to center. Exhale, slowly turn your head to the left.

- Inhale, return the head to center.

- Repeat two more times. After completing three rounds, pause, enjoying the quiet. Now, in the stillness of the breath, bring to your mind's eye a choice that you're about to make—today, this week, or this month. It can be a simple or large choice.

- Now invite SPIRE into your awareness. Examine your choice through the lens of each element of SPIRE. Remember to take long, deep breaths during this inquiry.

- Examine your choice from a spiritual, physical, and intellectual point of view, as well as from the relational and emotional perspectives. Whether you're choosing to begin something or choosing to end something, get a felt sense of that choice from within the framework of SPIRE.

- See what happens.

- Take a few more deep breaths.

- When you're ready, open your eyes. What did you learn?

Now you can go a step further: Using Let Your Yoga Dance, you can land some inSPIREd Positive Psychology teachings directly into the body. As you use your physical self to dance your yoga, you can simultaneously explore a fundamental spiritual quality of SPIRE: gratitude. When you embody gratitude your heart can open wider.

Practicing gratitude within the body is powerful medicine. Need proof? Simply dive into Professor Sonja Lyubomirsky's book *The How of Happiness*. Or read the work of Robert A. Emmons, a leading expert on gratitude and author of the books *Gratitude Works! Creating Emotional Prosperity: A 21-Day Program for Gratitude* and *Thanks! How the New Science of Gratitude Can Make You Happier*. Another great book on gratitude that I love is Brené Brown's *The Gifts of Imperfection*.

Brown, Emmons, and Lyubomirsky have written extensively on the power of gratitude and the research behind it. Positive Psychologists often recommend writing in a gratitude journal. I have kept a daily gratitude journal since the eighties. And yet, there is another way, a moving way, to practice gratitude. See what happens when you embody gratitude through the lens of the S and P of SPIRE, by letting your yoga dance.

LET'S MOVE!
Takeaway 14

Let Your Yoga Dance, with Gratitude
Dancing Mountain and Heart Warrior
Energy Booster

Put on your favorite piece of music, anything that moves you. My recommendations: Karen Drucker's "Thank You" from her lovely album, *The Heart of Healing*, or Sinead O'Connor's "Thank You" from her album *Universal Mother*.

This might be out of your comfort zone. Want to give it a try in private? You can't do this wrong, and you might even become surprised by joy.

- Standing or sitting, with your spine long and tall, enter slowly into Mountain pose. Feel your feet grounded on the earth, arms either resting down by your side, halfway up, or overhead. In Mountain, you're learning how to stand gracefully and strongly on your own two feet.

- Now begin to move your Mountain. Stretch your arms, wiggle your shoulders, bend and straighten your knees. Breathe deeply in through the nose, out through the mouth. Allow your body to be moved in this strong Mountain. Notice how you feel. Reaching your arms toward the sky, take a deep breath in, and then, as you exhale, bring your hands over your heart. Repeat these gestures many times: reaching for the sky, then reaching toward your heart.

Begin to think of three things for which you are grateful:

- Consider one thing about your body that you're grateful for. Be wholehearted in your gratefulness. Or think of a time your body went overboard to serve you. Or think of the many ways it has healed from injury, pain, or trauma.

- Now as you step your right leg forward into Warrior pose, with front knee bent, back leg straight, arms coming forward, think of someone in your life you're grateful for. Step back to Mountain. Forward into the Warrior, back to Mountain. Truly get a felt sense of this person as you continue to breathe deeply, sending gratitude from the depths of your heart.

- Next, as you switch to your left side, consider something in your life that you're grateful for. Breathe that gratitude in and out.

- As an added bonus, come back to yourself and name a quality about yourself that you value, appreciate, and love. Say it aloud. My favorite saying is: "I dance through life with grace and ease." It reminds me of all I aspire to.

- Keep moving your gratitude. You might even close your eyes and simply let your yoga dance by following your inner guidance.

When you feel complete, once again take some deep breaths, and ask yourself: How do I feel?

Doing this moving gratitude intervention can open your heart and expand your joy. Perhaps you can give yourself the gift of a Let Your Yoga Dance Gratitude Challenge: for five minutes every day for thirty days, play a favorite song, and dance your gratitude for someone or something. See what happens.

CHAPTER 6:

Dance Prayers
and
the Grace Garden of
Hearts and Souls

Dance Prayers

If you just practiced the LET'S MOVE Takeaway 14 at the end of the previous chapter, hopefully you're feeling some gratitude in this moment. Gratitude practice, as previously stated, is a hallmark of Positive Psychology and of Let Your Yoga Dance. Although it is a powerful positivity booster to speak or write our gratitude, I hope you have discovered that it is also compelling to move our gratitude by bringing it into the body. I will share with you some highlights, history, and healings from the Let Your Yoga Dance floor that have become an integral part of my practice of gratitude and embodied Positive Psychology.

History of Dance Prayers

The sixth chakra is often the place in class where gratitude magic happens. Dance Prayers contain moments of gratitude toward the end of each Let Your Yoga Dance class. Dance Prayers were born of my deepest sorrow, the death of my daughter, Sarah Grace, on August 8, 1995, stillborn at full term. Weeks after her birth, a touch of grace materialized in the form of a song that was given to me, a beautiful rendition of an old hymn, "Breathe on Me, Breath of God." The album, written by the group Miserable Offenders, was called, *Oh God Help Us*. It was deeply meaningful to me. I played the song continuously; I could not stop dancing. I swayed, I sighed, I prayed, I cried. Later, I discovered that certain dance movements had stayed with me: I actually had choreographed a moving prayer to this poignant music.

I realized that I could easily bring Dance Prayers to my students who, in turn, were profoundly moved. I observed that the quiet, inward focus toward the end of a Let Your Yoga Dance class was the perfect time to include a Dance Prayer. I found two ways to introduce them: One way was to lead choreography I had already created; another was to play a tender piece of music and invite the students to dance their own prayer. Since 1995, these Dance Prayers have become powerful, soulful, expressions of Grace and an integral part of the Let Your Yoga Dance experience. Because gratitude is so important in creating a joy-filled life, I have become a collector of gratitude songs.

Using Dance Prayers in Classes

There are many ways to use Dance Prayers effectively. For example, during longer workshops or trainings, I sometimes ask group members to create their own Dance Prayers in small circles of four. One person enters the circle, while the other three become compassionate witnesses. While heartfelt music plays, the dancer in the middle allows her body to become an instrument of prayer as the surrounding circle metaphorically holds her. She—or he—can pray or meditate, through movement, for her own well-being and for the ease and grace of all beings. The results can be breathtaking.

Dance Prayers are one of the most important aspects of my work because they provide an opportunity for students to connect with their indwelling spirit. Dance Prayers have nothing to do with a specific religion or path. They are created to allow us to retreat inside the self and return home to the movement within the stillness, and the stillness within the movement. Dance Prayers are a call to heal one's life and the lives of others.

The Grace Garden of Hearts and Souls

Healing happens.

How? Through trusting in Grace as divine, unmerited benediction. We don't have to work or struggle for Grace; we may not even deserve it! But sometimes it can wrap itself around us like a soft, tender blanket. Grace, also, can happen through my signature Dance Prayer: the Grace Garden of Hearts and Souls. I created this lovely experience decades ago to build loving, supportive community within the context of moving yoga.

I invite you now to get a felt sense of what happens in the Grace Garden. What follows is a transcription of an actual Garden group experience, including my guidance:

"To begin the Grace Garden experience, find a partner. Decide who will be the 'Heart' and who will be the 'Soul.' When ready, create two concentric circles: the inner standing circle is formed from Hearts; the outer standing circle, from Souls. Hearts, now transform your circle by walking into the center of the space to create a human sculpture by striking a yoga pose. Feel free to create a new yoga pose never seen before. Hearts, you may choose to sit—or lie—on the ground, to remain standing, or to reach toward the sky.

"The sculpting unfolds nonverbally, with soft, gentle music playing in the background.

"Souls, now come into the center to entwine the sculpture in, around, and through the Hearts. Souls, try to touch at least two other Hearts. In that touch—that connection between Hearts and Souls—realize that you are touching the ancestry of this being—parents, aunts, uncles, grandparents, great-grandparents—all the way back to the beginning of time.

"Hearts, when you are ready, step away from the sculpture.

"As the Hearts extricate themselves, the shell of the sculpture is left behind. The Souls are now alone and untouched in the middle of the formation. At this point, the Hearts rejoin the Sculpture, again touching, supporting, and enveloping the Souls, making sure no Soul is left alone.

"'Where am I needed?' and 'How can I serve?' Alternately, Hearts and Souls address these questions as they serve and support, exit and observe, while finding their place in a potentially precarious posture or a simple stance. A Heart might lie on the floor with her knees pulled into her chest. A Soul might slowly come to stand over this Heart, touching her shoulders.

"Now consider these questions, 'What happens if at some point you are not touched? What story are you going to make up about that?' This is an opportunity to learn to trust the 'touch of grace.'

"As we conclude the Grace Garden, let's gather together."

The clump of Hearts and Souls share their experience. Typical responses include:

"How can a bunch of strangers become so intimate?"

"I feel so taken care of."

"I forgot how much love there is in the world."

"I wish we could all do this together in New York at Ground Zero. In Congress. In the White House. In Israel. In Ukraine. In Syria. In Iraq. In prisons. In China. In Paris. Wherever refugees are. In my living room with friends and family."

I often use the Grace Garden to awaken the yoga dancer to the nature of grace and the dancer within. It is a spiritual practice with the intention of full self-expression through creative movement. This garden has gone far beyond my initial purpose and limited understanding. The outcome always is beyond words. The Grace Garden of Hearts and Souls sculpts the world, one heart and one soul at a time. It opens the door to the heart and soul by quickly breaking down barriers between people. Moments of grace can happen at any time in which the yoga dancer suddenly may be surprised, touched—even astonished—by joy and by the transformation of pain to insight.

Whether it elicits communal joy, poignant questioning, or tearful awakening, the intention of the Grace Garden is to serve one another, by both giving and by receiving. In this Garden, grace happens. Every single time. Because grace is not about pushing, striving, or controlling, dancers are free to relax and approach the experience with the wonder of a child. The Grace Garden is part of my daughter, Sarah Grace's, legacy—a legacy of loving-kindness that I offer to the world in her name and honor.

Healing Dance Prayers on September 11, 2001

On Tuesday, September 11, 2001, beginning at 8:30 a.m., my group of teacher trainees at Kripalu was exploring the sixth chakra. I had arranged a full morning of Dance Prayers for them—and for the whole world. Throughout the morning, the trainees in small groups were allowing themselves to see and be seen through the eyes of compassion. Tears were shed, prayers were danced. The room felt sacred, inspired, awe-filled. At 11:15 a.m., with thirty more minutes to go and the Dance Prayers still in progress, I was surprised to see one of my program assistants entering the room, ashen. When I asked what was wrong, she handed me a piece of paper. Somehow in the cacophony of words, I found the phrase: "The Twin Towers have fallen." It took me several moments to understand what had transpired. The words swirled in my head as I kept my eyes on my yoga dancers with their moving prayers. As I began to truly understand the cold horror of this dreadful news, I felt very protective of my innocent, unaware, praying dancers before me. I realized that their lives were about to be changed forever, and I was to be the bearer of the news. As I watched them in dancing prayer, I refused to interrupt. I knew they were doing great good for the Earth in those moments. I purposely waited until they were done.

Once we all had joined together, I told them of the horror occurring just three hours south of us. After some discussion and quiet, we decided, as a united group of thirty-five yoga dancers, to remain at Kripalu to complete the training. We trusted that our dance of yoga, our prayer, would hold us safely as we danced for the lost souls and their families in the midst of chaos and suffering. Dance Prayers helped us that morning, that week, and beyond, to process our loss and terror, to mourn for devastated families, and to acknowledge the grief of our nation and world. Dance Prayers were our grounding force, our light in the darkness. And so we moved on toward healing.

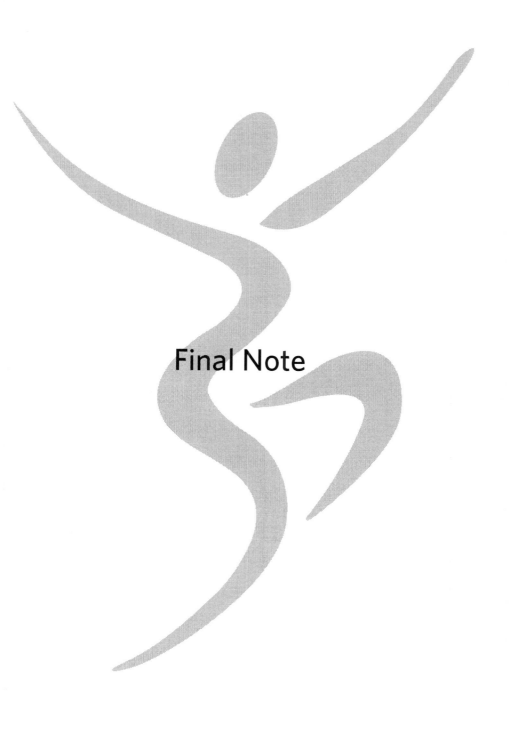

Final Note

*What we call the beginning
is often the end
And to make an end
Is to make a beginning.
The end is where we start from...*

—T. S. Eliot, The Four Quartets

Now it's time to return to the place where we started, and hopefully know the place for the first time:

You are a dancer.

I hope after reading this book you have become a believer!

Your body is more than something to make your head portable.

If you remember to practice the LET'S MOVE takeaways, you will never forget the magnificent wisdom of your body.

Expanding your joy is possible.

Having experienced and taught Let Your Yoga Dance in the Positive Psychology arena, the Special Populations arena, with the active population, with elders (or well-ders!), and with kids and teens for three decades now, I have witnessed wonders, both in my students and in myself. I have observed the unique ways in which different kinds of people benefit from letting their yoga dance. Businesspeople, grandparents, lawyers, therapists, pregnant moms, teens, toddlers, teachers, people with Parkinson's and MS, veterans, scholars, firefighters, doctors, nurses, yogis, professional dancers—all types of students have reported experiencing newfound joy in their bodies. Barbara Fredrickson's work in broadening and building positivity comes alive in the Let Your Yoga Dance practice. When we dance our yoga through the chakras, positivity does, in fact, build. Joy expands. This is not rocket science; it's common sense. One of my biggest learnings is that the practice of ongoing gratitude for the dance of this life—just as it is showing up in the present moment—is a practice to cherish.

My hope is that more and more people will experience the blending of embodied Positive Psychology with Let Your Yoga Dance. In this way, practitioners can find a sanctuary in which they feel held and soothed, while simultaneously rising to the height of their magnificence. They will also discover a psychology that invites their body into the mix, a psychology that respects and listens to the physical self, and all parts of the self. I consider this a great formula for joy.

I leave you with my surefire recipe for Expanding Joy 101:

Either alone with yourself, or with a group of any size, create a safe space where permission to be both human and magnificent is granted. Play music that touches body, heart, mind, and soul. Experiment with gentle movements that awaken the chakras. If you blend all these ingredients together, I can promise you that something unique will happen: an awakening to joy that will continue to expand, evolve, and grow. It is simply profound and profoundly simple.

So...

Let Your Yoga Dance
and
Expand your Joy!

Hakuna Matata!
Fewer Worries, Be Happier

References

Foreword

- Ben-Shahar, Tal. *Happier: the Secrets to Daily Joy and Lasting Fulfillment.* New York: McGraw Hill, 2007.

- Ben-Shahar, Tal. *Choose the Life You Want: The Mindful Way to Happiness.* New York: The Experiment. 2012.

Preface

- McDonough, Megan. *Radically Receptive Meditation: A Powerful Practice in Wide-Open Awareness.* Massachusetts: Wholebeing Institute. 2015.

Introduction

- Whitman, Walt. *Leaves of Grass.* Pennsylvania: David McKay, 1892.

- Lyubomirsky, Sonja. *The Myths of Happiness.* New York: Penguin Books. 2013. 127.

Chapter 1 – What is Let Your Yoga Dance

- Lovatt, Peter. "Psychology of Dance." TedxObserver. March, 2012. Lecture.

- Vergese, et al. "Leisure Activities and the Risk of Dementia in the Elderly." *New England Journal of Medicine:* 10.1056. 2003.

- Duberg et al. "Influencing self-rated health among adolescent girls with dance intervention: a randomized controlled trial." *Archives of Pediatrics and Adolescent Medicine* 2012. DOI: 10.1001/jamapediatrics.2013.421.

Chapter 2 – The Chakras

- Ben-Shahar, Tal. Video Lectures: Certificate in Positive Psychology, WholeBeing Institute. 2012.

- Cuddy, Amy. *Your Body Language Shapes Who You Are.* TED. June. 2012.

- Judith, Anodea & Vega, Selene. *The Sevenfold Journey: Reclaiming Body and Spirit through the Chakras.* California: The Crossing Press, 1993.

Chapter 3 - Yamas and Niyamas, Metta

- Boorstein, Sylvia. *Pay Attention, for Goodness Sake: Practicing the Perfections of the Heart—The Buddhist Path of Kindness.* New York: Ballantine Books, 2002.

Chapter 4 – Positive Psychology

- Ben-Shahar, Tal. *Being Happy*. New York: McGraw Hill. 2011.

- Seligman, Martin. *Flourish: A Visionary New Understanding of Happiness and Well-Being*. New York: Free Press. 2011.

- Tomasulo, Dan. "Maslow Revisited: The Hierarchy of Chakras?" *Psych Central*. 2011.

- Cain, Sue. *Quiet*. New York: Crown Publishers, 2012. 14.

- Norrish, Jacolyn. *Positive Education: The Geelong Grammar School Journey*. Oxford: Oxford University Press, 2015.

Chapter 5 – SPIRE

- Cooperrider, David L & Whtiney, Diana. *Appreciative Inquiry: A Positive Revolution in Change*. California. 2005.

- Csikszentmihalyi, Mihaly. *Flow: The Psychology of Optimal Experience*. New York: HarperCollins, 1990.

- Maslow, Abraham. "Toward a Positive Psychology." *Motivation and Personality*. 1954.

- Lyubomirsky, Sonya. *The How of Happiness*. New York: The Penguin Press, 2008.

- Emmons, Robert A. *Gratitude Works! A 21-Day Program for Creating Emotional Prosperity*. California: Jossey-Bass, 2013.

- Emmons, Robert A. *Thanks! How the New Science of Gratitude Can Make You Happier*. New York: Houghton Mifflin, 2007.

- Brown, Brené. *The Gifts of Imperfection*. Minnesota: Hazelton, 2010.

Chapter 6 - Dance Prayers and the Grace Garden

- Miserable Offenders. "Breathe on Me, Breath of God," Digital: *Oh God Help Us*. 1995.

Final Note

- Eliot, T. S. *The Four Quartets*. New York: Harcourt Publishing, Inc. 1943.

Gratitude

To all the teachers and students
in the Let Your Yoga Dance world community:

(I am including just a few folks here. If you don't see your name,
it's tucked inside my heart).

Irena Blethen, the Heart and Guardian of Let Your Yoga Dance;
Jyotika Jean Skeels; Andrea Cashman, Barbara Arnett; Stacey Clarfield Newman;
Anita Sanci; Elayna Bengal; Fern Westernoff; Lori Cable; Lisa Katz, Sho Albert;
Kelly Salasin; Diane Kovanda; Niti Seip Martin; Jurian Hughes; Rosemary Clough;
Noreen Kelty; Donna Miller; Ari Greenberg; Sue Bupp; Sheryl Sarnak;
Melissa Regan; Bonny Boice; Jeanne Griffin; Mark Pietuszka; Peggy Schjeldahl;
Heather Kravitz; Missy Brown, and the queen of gratitude, sanctuary,
and wise counsel: Elayne Goldstein.

Wholebeing Institute Colleagues:

Megan McDonough; Sonja Craig; Phoebe Atkinson; Fiona Trembath;
Maria Sirois; Rouben Madikians; Maria McManus, Nicole Stottlemeyer, and
Ruth Pearce (who still believes she's an introvert while dancing wildly).

My dance and spiritual teachers through the years:

Steffi Nossen; Pat Peterson; Vinn Arjuna Marti; Don Stapleton; Dan Leven;
Swami Kripalu; Sylvia Boorstein; S.N. Goenka; Amrit Desai; Pema Chrodron;
Angela Farmer; His Holiness the Dalai Lama.

My editor:

Jonathan Ambar, writer, coach, and burlesque dancer par excellence.
Thanks also to Tresca Weinstein for the read through.

Endless thanks to Tal.

I am so happy you love to let your yoga dance!

DVDs, CDs/Digital by Megha

- *Introduction to Yoga and Meditation DVD:* a great tool for both newcomers and those returning to yoga and meditation.

- *Moontides CD/Digital:* all-levels moving yoga, meditation, and chanting practice. Features the Moon Salutation.

- *Power and Grace CD/Digital:* dynamic yoga flow featuring variations on the Sun Salutation. Co-led with Devarshi Steven Hartman.

- *Animal Songs CD/Digital:* original songs about animals created and sung by Megha. Great for all ages. Known among listeners as "the feel-good album."

Dancing OM Logo

This little Dancing Om figure meanders through *Expanding Joy*. It was created for me by artist Bethann Shannon, and has been the logo for Let Your Yoga Dance since 1999. It was trademarked in 2007.

Info

If you would like to find a Let Your Yoga Dance class near you, or a workshop or training with me, please visit letyouryogadance.com. There are excellent Let Your Yoga Dance instructors teaching around the USA, Canada, and the world.

For more information about the Wholebeing institute and Positive Psychology, contact wholebeinginstitute.org

About the Author

Megha Nancy Buttenheim, M.A., E-RYT 1000, is Founding Director of *Let Your Yoga Dance® LLC.* A lifelong singer, dancer, and actor, she is a faculty member and teacher-trainer at Kripalu Center for Yoga & Health. She has led her own signature training, *Let Your Yoga Dance Teacher Training,* since 1997, in different parts of the world.

Megha is a faculty member with the Wholebeing Institute (WBI) and is the director of movement and meditation in WBI's Certificate in Positive Psychology, directed by Dr. Tal Ben-Shahar. For this program, she has created a new practice, Let Your Yoga Dance for Embodied Positive Psychology, which includes an Expanding Joy movement curriculum.

Megha's passion is to bring the dance of yoga to everyone, including special populations who feel marginalized due to age, Parkinson's, Alzheimer's, MS, and other health conditions. To that end, Megha directs Let Your Yoga Dance Teacher Training for Special Populations. She also teaches Let Your Yoga Dance for Parkinson's with the support of Garden of the Heart Yoga and NeuroChallenge of Sarasota, Florida.

Please visit letyouryogadance.com for more information—or conversation—with Megha.